Better Homes and Gardens®

30-MINUTE main dishes

COOKING FOR TODAY

BETTER HOMES AND GARDENS® BOOKS
Des Moines

BETTER HOMES AND GARDENS® BOOKS
An Imprint of Meredith® Books

30-MINUTE MAIN DISHES
Editor: Mary Major Williams
Copy Chief: Gregory H. Kayko
Associate Art Director: Tom Wegner
Writer: Marcia K. Stanley
Copy Editor: Kathleen Poole
Indexer: Kathleen Poole
Electronic Production Coordinator: Paula Forest
Test Kitchen Product Supervisors: Diana Nolin, Colleen Weeden
Food Stylists: Lynn Blanchard, Janet Pittman, Jennifer Peterson
Photographers: Mike Dieter, Scott Little
Cover Photographer: Andy Lyons
Production Manager: Douglas Johnston

Director, New Product Development: Ray Wolf
Managing Editor: Christopher Cavanaugh
Test Kitchen Director: Sharon Stilwell

Meredith Publishing Group
President, Publishing Group: Christopher Little
Vice President and Publishing Director: John P. Loughlin

Meredith Corporation
Chairman of the Board and Chief Executive Officer: Jack D. Rehm
President and Chief Operating Officer: William T. Kerr

Chairman of the Executive Committee: E. T. Meredith III

On the cover: Apricot Pork Medaillions (see recipe, page 30)

All of us at Better Homes and Gardens® Books are dedicated to providing you with the information and ideas you need to create delicious foods. We welcome your comments and suggestions. Write to us at: Better Homes and Gardens® Books, Cookbook Editorial Department, RW-240, 1716 Locust St., Des Moines, IA 50309-3023

If you would like to order additional copies of any of our books, call 1-800-678-2803 or check with your local bookstore.

Our seal assures you that every recipe in *30-Minute Main Dishes* has been tested in the Better Homes and Gardens® Test Kitchen. This means that each recipe is practical and reliable, and meets our high standards of taste appeal. We guarantee your satisfaction with this book for as long as you own it.

Short on time, but long on hunger? It's a typical problem at mealtime all across the country. Even though your schedules may be busier than ever, your family still needs to eat. This collection of 68 mouthwatering main dishes solves that mealtime dilemma. Each recipe was developed and tested in the Better Homes and Gardens® Test Kitchen to be prepared from start to finish in 30 minutes or less, and still meet your family's high standards for great taste.

Whether you need a quick meal to feed the kids before soccer practice or a company-special dinner for last minute guests, you'll find the perfect recipe on these pages. From hearty Hot Turkey Sub Sandwiches to elegant Beef Tenderloins with Wine Sauce, this book offers a variety of tantalizing main dishes to star at sumptuous meals.

As every busy cook knows, the actual cooking of the meals is only half the battle; the other half is organization. To further help you out, we've included tips on everything from grocery shopping to fast-cooking strategies. Use these hints along with our recipes and you'll be serving great-tasting meals in minutes.

CONTENTS

GROCERY-SHOPPING SAVVY

No one likes to fight their way through busy grocery store aisles night after night. It uses your limited time and leaves you feeling frazzled. With a little organization you can avoid that hassle. To help you out, here are some of our best grocery shopping hints.

■ Shop just once a week. One well-organized trip to the grocery store each week saves time as well as money.

■ Make a list. Keep paper and pencil handy in your kitchen and remind family members to add items they notice need replenishing.

■ Organize your grocery list. Group items on your list according to the grocery store's floor plan. This eliminates unnecessary backtracking.

■ Use the same in-store route every time you shop. The routine will help you organize your grocery list and reduce your shopping time.

■ Shop when others don't. Try early morning or late evening hours. By avoiding busy times, you'll miss crowded aisles and long waits at the check-out lines.

■ Take of advantage of "stores within a store." You can fill prescriptions, buy flowers, drop off dry cleaning, rent videos, and mail packages at many grocery stores. Use these services and avoid driving from one merchant to another.

TIME-SAVING PRODUCTS

Everyone's busy these days and food companies know it. As a result, you'll find more good-quality convenience products on your supermarket's shelves than ever before. Listed below is a sampling of some of our favorites.

■ Sliced fresh mushrooms
■ Pre-washed spinach
■ Ready-to-eat peeled baby carrots
■ Packaged shredded cabbage with carrot (coleslaw mix)
■ Packaged torn mixed salad greens
■ Cleaned and cut-up broccoli flowerets
■ Cleaned and cut-up cauliflower flowerets
■ Bottled minced garlic
■ Cleaned and cut-up melons
■ Peeled and cut-up fresh pineapple
■ Canned tomato products with added seasonings
■ Quick-cooking rice and noodle mixes
■ Dry soup and sauce mixes

■ Cornflake crumbs
■ Cooked and deveined fresh shrimp
■ Sliced chicken, poultry, and beef for stir-frying
■ Marinated chicken breasts
■ Roasted chicken
■ Frozen vegetable and pasta mixtures with seasonings
■ Frozen mashed potatoes
■ Finely shredded fresh Parmesan cheese
■ Refrigerated pasta
■ Deli salads
■ Deli dips and spreads
■ Cooked poultry, beef, and ham
■ Baked and decorated cakes

CHOPPING SHORTCUTS

These tips will speed up the tedious job of chopping ingredients.
- Keep your knives sharp. It's much easier and faster to chop vegetables with a sharp knife than it is with a dull one.
- Clean and chop vegetables in advance and all at once. You'll have just one mess to clean up and vegetables will be ready to use when needed.
- When a recipe calls for 1 medium onion (½ cup), don't bother measuring it. A little more or a little less won't hurt your recipe.

FAST-COOKING STRATEGIES

All the recipes in this book are quick, but if you follow these tips you'll shave minutes off your preparation time.
- Turn on the oven or broiler first. It will be preheated when you need it.
- Purchase food in the form specified in the recipe. Buying shredded cheese, boned chicken breasts, or bottled minced garlic saves cooking time and effort.
- Overlap preparation steps. While waiting for water to boil or meat to brown, start chopping vegetables, opening cans, or mixing a filling.
- Choose a baking dish that will double as a serving dish. It saves on clean-up time, too.
- Rinse dishes and load them into the dishwasher or set them aside as you cook. Food won't have time to dry on the dishes, so your after-meal clean-up will be easier.
- Involve all the family members in cooking. Divide the jobs so each person works in their own area to avoid bumping into one another.

EASY BROILER CLEAN-UP

Make grimy broiler pans a thing of the past. Line your broiler pan with foil and spray the unheated rack with nonstick spray coating. It makes clean-up a snap. Just wash the rack in hot soapy water. The nonstick coating reduces any needed scrubbing. And cleaning the pan is even easier. Just remove the foil, wad it up, and throw it out.

TENDERLOINS WITH ROSEMARY AND MUSHROOMS

Serve these savory steaks with a packaged salad mix, steamed asparagus spears, and purchased dinner rolls for a speedy yet elegant meal.

1   tablespoon margarine or butter
1   tablespoon cooking oil
4   beef tenderloin steaks, cut 1-inch
    thick
2   cups sliced fresh mushrooms
2   green onions, sliced (¼ cup)
1   tablespoon snipped fresh rosemary or
    1 teaspoon dried rosemary, crushed
½   teaspoon bottled minced garlic
¼   teaspoon pepper
⅓   cup dry sherry, dry red wine, or beef
    broth
    Fresh rosemary sprigs (optional)

In a large skillet melt margarine or butter. Stir in cooking oil. Trim any separable fat from steaks. Add steaks to skillet and cook over medium to medium-high heat for 10 to 12 minutes or to desired doneness, turning once. Transfer to a serving platter, reserving drippings in skillet. Keep steaks warm.

Stir mushrooms, green onions, rosemary, garlic, and pepper into reserved drippings. Cook and stir over medium-high heat for 3 to 4 minutes or till mushrooms are tender. Reduce heat. Carefully stir in sherry, wine, or beef broth. Cook and stir about 1 minute more or till heated through. Spoon over steaks. Garnish with fresh rosemary sprigs, if desired. Makes 4 servings.

Nutrition facts per serving: 249 calories, 14 g total fat (4 g saturated fat), 64 mg cholesterol, 83 mg sodium, 4 g carbohydrate, 1 g fiber, 23 g protein.
Daily Value: 4% vitamin A, 5% vitamin C, 1% calcium, 24% iron.

HOT ITALIAN BEEF SALAD

For a reduced-fat version of this flavorful salad, use a fat-free Italian salad dressing. You'll cut the fat by a whopping 18 grams.

¾ **pound beef flank steak or beef top round steak, cut 1-inch thick**

6 **cups packaged torn mixed salad greens**

3 **teaspoons olive oil or cooking oil**

1 **medium red or green sweet pepper, cut into bite-size strips (¾ cup)**

½ **cup clear Italian salad dressing or red wine vinegar and oil salad dressing**

1 **tablespoon grated Parmesan cheese Coarsely ground pepper**

Trim any separable fat from beef. Cut beef into thin bite-size strips. Arrange the salad greens on 4 salad plates.

In a large skillet heat *2 teaspoons* of the oil. Add the red or green pepper and cook for 1 to 2 minutes or till nearly crisp-tender.

Add the remaining 1 teaspoon oil to the skillet. Add beef. Cook and stir for 2 to 3 minutes or to desired doneness. Add salad dressing. Cook and stir till heated through. Spoon the beef mixture over the salad greens. Sprinkle with Parmesan cheese and pepper. Serve immediately. Makes 4 servings.

Nutrition facts per serving: 318 calories, 24 g total fat (5 g saturated fat), 41 mg cholesterol, 348 mg sodium, 7 g carbohydrate, 2 g fiber, 19 g protein. Daily Value: 44% vitamin A, 74% vitamin C, 6% calcium, 19% iron.

EASY SHEPHERD'S PIE

Frozen mashed potatoes make quick work of this family-style skillet supper.

1   22-ounce package frozen mashed
      potatoes
1¾ cups milk
1   10-ounce package (2 cups) frozen
      mixed vegetables
1   pound ground beef, ground raw
      turkey, or ground raw chicken
¼   cup water
1   teaspoon dried minced onion
1   10¾-ounce can condensed tomato
      soup or one 10¾-ounce can
      reduced-sodium condensed
      tomato soup
1   teaspoon Worcestershire sauce
¼   teaspoon dried thyme, crushed
½   cup shredded cheddar cheese
      (2 ounces)

Prepare potatoes according to package directions using *4 cups* of the frozen potatoes and the milk. Meanwhile, run cold water over frozen mixed vegetables to separate. In a large skillet cook ground beef, turkey, or chicken over medium-high heat till no longer pink. Drain off any fat.

Stir in vegetables, water, and onion. Bring to boiling. Reduce heat. Cover and simmer for 5 to 10 minutes or till vegetables are tender. Stir in soup, Worcestershire sauce, and thyme. Return to boiling. Drop potatoes in mounds on top of the hot mixture. Sprinkle with cheese. Reduce heat. Cover and simmer about 5 minutes more or till heated through. Makes 6 servings.

Nutrition facts per serving: 342 calories, 16 g total fat (7 g saturated fat), 62 mg cholesterol, 541 mg sodium, 30 g carbohydrate, 1 g fiber, 19 g protein. Daily Value: 24% vitamin A, 25% vitamin C, 7% calcium, 13% iron.

BARBECUED BEEF SANDWICHES

Slices of peppery cheese top saucy beef strips in these robust sandwiches.

¾ pound beef sirloin steak or beef top
    round steak, cut 1-inch thick
1 medium onion, sliced and separated
    into rings
1 tablespoon cooking oil
⅔ cup barbecue sauce
1 teaspoon lemon juice or vinegar
4 hoagie buns, split and toasted
4 slices Monterey Jack cheese with
    jalapeño peppers or Monterey Jack
    cheese
    Fresh chili peppers (optional)

Trim any separable fat from beef. Cut into bite-size strips.

In a large skillet cook onion in hot oil over medium-high heat about 3 minutes or till tender. Add beef strips. Cook and stir for 2 to 3 minutes or to desired doneness.

Stir in barbecue sauce and lemon juice or vinegar. Cook over medium heat till heated through, stirring occasionally. Spoon beef mixture onto hoagie bun bottoms. Top with cheese slices and then bun tops. Serve with fresh chili peppers, if desired. Makes 4 servings.

Nutrition facts per serving: 692 calories, 22 g total fat (9 g saturated fat), 76 mg cholesterol, 1256 mg sodium, 83 g carbohydrate, 5 g fiber, 38 g protein. Daily Value: 10% vitamin A, 7% vitamin C, 19% calcium, 38% iron.

BEEF TENDERLOINS WITH WINE SAUCE

Had a great day at work and feel like celebrating? Serve these richly sauced steaks for dinner.

4 **beef tenderloin steaks, cut 1-inch thick**
½ **teaspoon coarsely cracked pepper**
1 **tablespoon margarine or butter**
½ **of a medium onion, chopped (¼ cup)**
¼ **cup beef broth**
¼ **cup dry red wine**
1 **teaspoon dried marjoram, crushed**

Trim any separable fat from steaks. Press pepper onto both sides of steaks. In a large skillet cook steaks in hot margarine or butter over medium to medium-high heat for 10 to 12 minutes or to desired doneness, turning once. Transfer steaks to a serving platter, reserving drippings in skillet. Keep steaks warm while preparing sauce.

For sauce, stir onion into reserved drippings in skillet. Cook for 3 to 4 minutes or till onion is tender. Remove from heat. Carefully add broth, wine, and marjoram to onion in skillet, stirring to scrape up any browned bits. Return to heat. Bring to boiling. Reduce heat. Boil gently, uncovered, about 2 minutes or till mixture is reduced to about ¼ cup. Serve sauce over steaks. Makes 4 servings.

Nutrition facts per serving: 315 calories, 15 g total fat (5 g saturated fat), 112 mg cholesterol, 176 mg sodium, 2 g carbohydrate, 0 g fiber, 38 g protein.
***Daily Value:** 3% vitamin A, 1% vitamin C, 1% calcium, 33% iron.*

BURGER OPTIONS

Choose salsa and Monterey Jack cheese for a Mexican burger, pizza sauce and mozzarella cheese for an Italian burger, or chutney and cheddar cheese for an Indian-style burger.

2   **tablespoons fine dry bread crumbs**
2   **tablespoons salsa, pizza sauce, or snipped chutney**
¼   **teaspoon salt**
⅛   **teaspoon pepper**
1   **pound lean ground beef or ground pork**
4   **slices Monterey Jack, mozzarella, cheddar, American, or Swiss cheese (optional)**
4   **kaiser rolls or hamburger buns, split and toasted**
4   **lettuce leaves**
    Salsa, pizza sauce, or chutney (optional)

In a medium mixing bowl stir together bread crumbs; the 2 tablespoons salsa, pizza sauce, or chutney; salt; and pepper. Add ground beef or pork. Mix well. Shape into four ¾-inch-thick patties.

Place patties on the unheated rack of a broiler pan. Broil 4 to 5 inches from the heat for 12 to 14 minutes or till no longer pink, turning once. Top with cheese slices during the last 1 minute of broiling, if desired.

Serve on kaiser rolls or hamburger buns with lettuce leaves, and, if desired, additional salsa, pizza sauce, or chutney. Makes 4 servings.

Nutrition facts per serving: 339 calories, 16 g total fat (6 g saturated fat), 71 mg cholesterol, 422 mg sodium, 22 g carbohydrate, 1 g fiber, 25 g protein. Daily Value: 0% vitamin A, 3% vitamin C, 3% calcium, 20% iron.

GARLIC-MUSTARD STEAK SANDWICHES

Another time, skip the hoagie rolls and serve the zesty steak strips with fresh tomato slices, corn-on-the-cob, and a tossed green salad.

2 tablespoons Dijon-style mustard
½ teaspoon dried marjoram or thyme, crushed
½ teaspoon bottled minced garlic
¼ teaspoon coarsely ground pepper
1 to 1½ pounds beef flank steak
4 hoagie rolls, split
  Dijon-style mustard (optional)

In a small mixing bowl stir together the 2 tablespoons mustard, marjoram or thyme, garlic, and pepper. Trim any separable fat from the steak. Brush both sides of the steak with the mustard mixture.

Place the steak on the unheated rack of a broiler pan. Broil 4 to 5 inches from the heat for 12 to 17 minutes or to desired doneness, turning once. Thinly slice steak diagonally across the grain. Serve steak strips in hoagie rolls. Pass additional mustard, if desired. Makes 4 to 6 servings.

Nutrition facts per serving: 176 calories, 9 g total fat (3 g saturated fat), 53 mg cholesterol, 255 mg sodium, 1 g carbohydrate, 0 g fiber, 22 g protein.
***Daily Value:** 0% vitamin A, 0% vitamin C, 0% calcium, 14% iron.*

ITALIAN BEEF SOUP

Keep the ingredients on hand for this easy soup and you'll always be prepared to whip up a hearty supper.

1 **pound ground beef**
2 **14½-ounce cans beef broth**
3 **cups frozen pasta with broccoli, corn, and carrots in garlic seasoned sauce**
1 **16-ounce can diced tomatoes**
1 **5½-ounce can tomato juice or ⅔ cup no-salt-added tomato juice**
2 **teaspoons dried Italian seasoning, crushed**
¼ **cup grated Parmesan cheese**

In a large saucepan cook beef till no longer pink. Drain off fat.

Add beef broth, pasta with mixed vegetables, *undrained* tomatoes, tomato juice, and Italian seasoning to beef in saucepan. Bring to boiling. Reduce heat. Simmer, uncovered, about 10 minutes or till vegetables and pasta are tender. Ladle into soup bowls. Sprinkle with Parmesan cheese. Makes 6 servings.

Nutrition facts per serving: 258 calories, 14 g total fat (6 g saturated fat), 54 mg cholesterol, 929 mg sodium, 13 g carbohydrate, 1 g fiber, 20 g protein. **Daily Value:** *19% vitamin A, 23% vitamin C, 8% calcium, 18% iron.*

HERBED STEAK

Enjoy this delicious steak in the summertime. For optimal flavor, use a vine-ripened tomato and fresh herbs.

2   beef top loin steaks, cut ¾-inch thick
       (about 1¼ pounds total)
1   tablespoon margarine or butter
3   green onions, sliced (about ⅓ cup)
1½   teaspoons snipped fresh thyme or
       basil or ½ teaspoon dried thyme
       or basil, crushed
¼   teaspoon salt
⅛   teaspoon pepper
1   medium tomato, chopped (⅔ cup)
       Fresh basil or thyme (optional)

Trim separable fat from steaks. Cut each steak in half. In a large heavy skillet cook steaks in hot margarine or butter over medium heat about 10 minutes or to desired doneness, turning once.

Remove steaks, reserving drippings in skillet. Keep steaks warm. Cook green onions, thyme or basil, salt, and pepper in drippings for 1 to 2 minutes or till green onions are tender. Stir in tomato. Heat through. Spoon over steaks. Garnish with fresh basil or thyme, if desired. Makes 4 servings.

Nutrition facts per serving: 207 calories, 9 g total fat (3 g saturated fat), 81 mg cholesterol, 230 mg sodium, 2 g carbohydrate, 0 g fiber, 28 g protein.
Daily Value: 7% vitamin A, 12% vitamin C, 1% calcium, 21% iron.

TORTELLINI WITH MEAT SAUCE

For a spicier sauce, replace the ground beef or pork with bulk Italian sausage.

½   pound ground beef or ground pork
1   14-ounce jar tomato and herb pasta
      sauce or spaghetti sauce
1¾ cups water
¼   cup dry red wine or water
1   9-ounce package refrigerated cheese-
      filled tortellini or half of a
      16-ounce package frozen cheese-
      filled tortellini
½   cup shredded mozzarella cheese
      (2 ounces)

In a large saucepan cook ground beef or pork over medium heat till no longer pink. Drain off fat.

Add pasta or spaghetti sauce, 1¾ cups water, and ¼ cup wine or water to the meat in the saucepan. Bring to boiling. Stir in refrigerated or frozen tortellini. Return to boiling. Simmer, uncovered, for 15 to 18 minutes or till tortellini are tender and sauce is of desired consistency. Spoon onto serving plates. Sprinkle with shredded mozzarella cheese. Let stand for 2 to 3 minutes or till cheese is melted. Makes 4 servings.

Nutrition facts per serving: 528 calories, 20 g total fat (6 g saturated fat), 62 mg cholesterol, 1224 mg sodium, 54 g carbohydrate, 2 g fiber, 28 g protein. Daily Value: 19% vitamin A, 26% vitamin C, 27% calcium, 18% iron.

ORIENTAL BEEF AND NOODLES

Want more Oriental flavor? Substitute ¼ teaspoon of five-spice powder for the ground ginger.

1   3-ounce package Oriental noodles
    with beef flavor
½   pound beef sirloin steak, cut ¾-inch
    thick
1   tablespoon cooking oil
1   medium carrot, thinly sliced (½ cup)
1   stalk celery, bias-sliced (½ cup)
1   6-ounce package frozen pea pods,
    thawed
¼   cup water
1   tablespoon snipped fresh parsley
2   teaspoons teriyaki sauce
½   teaspoon ground ginger
¼   teaspoon crushed red pepper
    (optional)

Cook Oriental noodles according to package directions, *except* drain the noodles and reserve the seasoning package.

Meanwhile, trim separable fat from the steak. Cut the steak into thin bite-size strips; set aside.

Pour the oil into a wok or large skillet. (Add more oil as necessary during cooking.) Heat over medium-high heat. Add carrot and celery. Stir-fry for 2 to 3 minutes or till crisp-tender. Remove the vegetables from the wok.

Add the steak strips to the hot wok. Stir-fry for 2 to 3 minutes or to desired doneness. Return carrot and celery to the wok. Stir in noodles, reserved seasoning package, pea pods, water, parsley, teriyaki sauce, ginger, and, if desired, crushed red pepper. Cook over medium heat till heated through, stirring occasionally. Makes 3 servings.

Nutrition facts per serving: 621 calories, 30 g total fat (3 g saturated fat), 50 mg cholesterol, 1724 mg sodium, 61 g carbohydrate, 2 g fiber, 30 g protein. Daily Value: 69% vitamin A, 33% vitamin C, 5% calcium, 29% iron.

SOUTHWEST BEEF-LINGUINE TOSS

A jar of picante sauce makes an easy, yet flavor-packed sauce in this stir-fried dish.

4 ounces linguine
¾ pound beef top round steak
1 tablespoon cooking oil
2 teaspoons chili powder
½ teaspoon bottled minced garlic
1 small onion, sliced and separated
    into rings
1 red or green sweet pepper,
    cut into strips
1 10-ounce package frozen whole
    kernel corn
¼ cup picante sauce
   Fresh cilantro (optional)

Cook linguine according to package directions. Drain. Rinse with warm water. Set aside.

Meanwhile, trim any separable fat from beef. Cut beef into thin, bite-size strips. Set aside.

Pour cooking oil into a wok or large skillet. (Add more oil as necessary during cooking.) Heat over medium-high heat. Stir-fry chili powder and garlic in hot oil for 15 seconds. Add onion; stir-fry for 1 minute. Add the red or green pepper; stir-fry for 1 to 2 minutes more or till vegetables are crisp-tender. Remove vegetables from the wok.

Add the beef to the hot wok; stir-fry for 2 to 3 minutes or to desired doneness. Return vegetables to the wok. Add corn and picante sauce. Stir the ingredients together. Add the cooked linguine. Toss all ingredients together to coat with picante sauce. Cook and stir till heated through. Garnish with fresh cilantro, if desired. Makes 4 servings.

Nutrition facts per serving: 351 calories, 9 g total fat (2 g saturated fat), 54 mg cholesterol, 166 mg sodium, 43 g carbohydrate, 1 g fiber, 27 g protein. **Daily Value:** *20% vitamin A, 68% vitamin C, 1% calcium, 25% iron.*

APRICOT PORK MEDAILLIONS

The tangy apricot sauce enhances the mild flavor of the fork-tender pork. (Also pictured on the cover.)

1   cup quick-cooking rice
¾   pound pork tenderloin
1   tablespoon margarine or butter
1   16-ounce can unpeeled apricot halves
      in light syrup
1   tablespoon cornstarch
¼   cup red plum jam or currant jelly
2   tablespoons white wine vinegar
2   green onions, sliced (¼ cup)

Cook rice according to package directions. Meanwhile, trim separable fat from pork. Cut into ¾-inch-thick slices. With a meat mallet, pound each slice between plastic wrap to ½-inch thickness.

In a large skillet cook pork in margarine or butter over medium-high heat for 4 to 6 minutes or till no longer pink, turning once. Remove pork from skillet. Keep warm.

Meanwhile, for sauce, drain apricots, reserving ⅔ cup of the juice. Set juice aside. Cut apricot pieces in half. In a small saucepan stir together reserved apricot juice and cornstarch. Stir in plum jam or currant jelly and vinegar. Cook and stir over medium heat till thickened and bubbly. Cook and stir for 2 minutes more. Stir in apricots. Heat through.

Divide rice among 4 dinner plates. Top with pork medaillions. Spoon sauce over pork. Sprinkle with green onions. Makes 4 servings.

Nutrition facts per serving: 341 calories, 6 g total fat (2 g saturated fat), 60 mg cholesterol, 85 mg sodium, 50 g carbohydrate, 2 g fiber, 21 g protein. **Daily Value:** *24% vitamin A, 11% vitamin C, 2% calcium, 17% iron.*

EASY MOO-SHU-STYLE PORK

For an easy garnish, save some of the shredded carrot from the coleslaw mix.

8   7-inch flour tortillas
3   tablespoons water
2   tablespoons soy sauce
1   tablespoon cornstarch
2   teaspoons toasted sesame oil
1   teaspoon sugar
¼   teaspoon bottled minced garlic
¾   pound pork tenderloin or pork loin
1   tablespoon cooking oil
3   cups packaged shredded cabbage with
      carrot (coleslaw mix)
⅓   cup hoisin sauce
      Carrot shreds (optional)
      Cherry tomatoes, quartered (optional)

Wrap tortillas in foil. Warm in a 350° oven for 10 minutes. Meanwhile, for sauce, in a small mixing bowl stir together water, soy sauce, cornstarch, sesame oil, sugar, and garlic. Set aside.

Trim separable fat from pork. Cut into thin bite-size strips. Pour cooking oil into a wok or large skillet. (Add more oil as necessary during cooking.) Heat over medium-high heat. Stir-fry the pork for 2 to 3 minutes or till no longer pink.

Push meat from the center of the wok. Stir sauce. Add to the center of the wok. Cook and stir till thickened and bubbly. Cook and stir for 2 minutes more. Add shredded cabbage with carrot to skillet. Stir ingredients together to coat with sauce.

Spread one side of each warm tortilla with some of the hoisin sauce. Spoon about *½ cup* of the pork mixture in the center of *each* tortilla. Fold bottom edge up over filling. Fold sides to the center, overlapping edges. Secure with wooden toothpicks. Garnish with carrot and cherry tomatoes, if desired. Makes 4 servings.

Nutrition facts per serving: 435 calories, 14 g total fat (3 g saturated fat), 60 mg cholesterol, 2266 mg sodium, 49 g carbohydrate, 1 g fiber, 27 g protein. Daily Value: 39% vitamin A, 47% vitamin C, 10% calcium, 29% iron.

ITALIAN PORK SANDWICHES

For added pizzazz, cook the pork as directed, then cook some chopped onion and chopped green sweet pepper in the skillet. Stir in the Italian cooking sauce and continue as directed.

¾ **pound pork tenderloin**
¼ **cup fine dry seasoned bread crumbs**
1 **tablespoon margarine or butter**
½ **cup Italian cooking sauce, spaghetti sauce, or pizza sauce**
4 **kaiser rolls or hamburger buns, split**
2 **tablespoons grated Parmesan cheese**

Cut pork crosswise into 4 slices. With a meat mallet, pound each slice between plastic wrap to ¼-inch thickness. Place seasoned bread crumbs in a shallow bowl. Dip each pork slice into the bread crumbs, coating lightly.

In a large skillet cook 2 pork slices in hot margarine or butter for 6 to 8 minutes or till pork is no longer pink, turning once. Remove from skillet. Keep warm. Repeat with remaining pork, adding more margarine or butter, if necessary.

Add Italian cooking sauce, spaghetti sauce, or pizza sauce to skillet. Cook and stir till heated through. Place each pork slice on the bottom of a roll or bun. Spoon some sauce over each. Sprinkle each with Parmesan cheese; add tops of rolls or buns. Makes 4 servings.

Nutrition facts per serving: 605 calories, 13 g total fat (4 g saturated fat), 70 mg cholesterol, 1279 mg sodium, 86 g carbohydrate, 17 g fiber, 34 g protein.
Daily Value: 10% vitamin A, 9% vitamin C, 10% calcium, 29% iron.

PORK AND NOODLE SKILLET DINNER

Strips of boneless chicken breast or thighs taste equally delicious in this creamy one-dish meal.

¾ **pound lean boneless pork**
1 **medium onion, chopped (½ cup)**
1 **tablespoon cooking oil**
3 **cups frozen loose-pack broccoli,**
  cauliflower, and carrots
4 **ounces medium noodles or curly**
  medium noodles (3 cups)
1 **10¾-ounce can reduced-sodium**
  condensed cream of celery soup
1 **cup reduced-sodium chicken broth**
¾ **cup water**
½ **teaspoon dried marjoram or thyme,**
  crushed
¼ **teaspoon pepper**

Trim separable fat from pork. Cut pork into thin bite-size strips. In a 12-inch skillet cook and stir pork and onion in hot oil over medium-high heat for 3 to 4 minutes or till pork is no longer pink.

Stir in frozen vegetables, noodles, soup, broth, water, marjoram or thyme, and pepper. Bring to boiling. Reduce heat. Cover and simmer for 12 to 15 minutes or till noodles are tender, stirring occasionally. Makes 4 servings.

Nutrition facts per serving: 317 calories, 12 g total fat (3 g saturated fat), 64 mg cholesterol, 531 mg sodium, 33 g carbohydrate, 3 g fiber, 19 g protein.
Daily Value: 108% vitamin A, 55% vitamin C, 4% calcium, 14% iron.

PORK WITH RHUBARB SAUCE

A tangy rhubarb sauce perks up these succulent pork chops.

4   boneless pork loin chops,
         cut ¾-inch thick
      Salt
      Pepper
½   cup apple juice
1   tablespoon cornstarch
1   tablespoon brown sugar
⅛   teaspoon ground ginger
1   cup frozen unsweetened sliced
         rhubarb

Trim separable fat from chops. Place chops on the *unheated* rack of a broiler pan. Sprinkle with salt and pepper. Broil 3 to 4 inches from the heat for 8 to 14 minutes or till no longer pink and juices run clear, turning chops over after half of the broiling time.

Meanwhile, for sauce, in a small saucepan stir together apple juice, cornstarch, brown sugar, and ginger. Stir in rhubarb. Cook and stir over medium heat till thickened and bubbly. Cook and stir for 2 minutes more.

To serve, place chops on a serving plate. Spoon some of the sauce over each chop. Pass remaining sauce. Makes 4 servings.

Nutrition facts per serving: 200 calories, 10 g total fat (3 g saturated fat), 59 mg cholesterol, 116 mg sodium, 10 g carbohydrate, 1 g fiber, 18 g protein. **Daily Value:** *0% vitamin A, 5% vitamin C, 3% calcium, 5% iron.*

SHERRIED PORK

Just add steamed baby carrots and peas and a loaf of crusty French bread for an elegant dining experience.

¾ **pound pork tenderloin**
1 **beaten egg**
1 **tablespoon milk**
½ **cup cornflake crumbs**
⅛ **teaspoon garlic powder**
2 **tablespoons margarine or butter**
¼ **cup water**
¼ **cup dry sherry, dry marsala, or water**
1 **teaspoon instant chicken bouillon**
   granules
   Dash pepper
1 **tablespoon snipped fresh parsley**

Trim any separable fat from pork. Cut pork crosswise into 4 pieces. With a meat mallet pound each slice between plastic wrap to ¼-inch thickness. In a shallow bowl combine egg and milk. In another bowl combine cornflake crumbs and garlic powder. Dip each pork slice into the egg mixture. Then dip into the crumb mixture, coating well.

In a large skillet cook pork slices in the hot margarine or butter for 6 to 8 minutes or till pork is no longer pink, turning once. Remove from skillet. Keep warm.

Stir the ¼ cup water; the ¼ cup sherry, marsala, or water; bouillon granules; and pepper into the drippings in the skillet, scraping up any browned bits. Bring to boiling. Boil rapidly for 2 to 3 minutes or till mixture thickens slightly. Serve over pork slices. Sprinkle with parsley. Makes 4 servings.

Nutrition facts per serving: 224 calories, 10 g total fat (3 g saturated fat), 114 mg cholesterol, 416 mg sodium, 7 g carbohydrate, 0 g fiber, 21 g protein.
Daily Value: *17% vitamin A, 7% vitamin C, 1% calcium, 11% iron.*

HAM AND SWISS PIZZA

In this simple recipe, traditional sandwich ingredients reconfigure into a family-pleasing pizza.

1 green sweet pepper, cut into bite-size
    strips (¾ cup)
1 small onion, sliced and separated into
    rings (⅓ cup)
1 tablespoon olive oil or cooking oil
1 tablespoon Dijon-style mustard or
    coarse brown mustard
½ teaspoon caraway seed, crushed
1 16-ounce package Boboli
    (12-inch Italian bread shell)
6 ounces fully cooked ham, cut into
    thin strips
1 cup cherry tomatoes, halved
1 cup shredded Swiss cheese (4 ounces)

In a large skillet cook green pepper and onion in hot oil for 2 to 3 minutes or till tender. Stir in mustard and caraway seed. Set aside.

Place bread shell on a lightly greased baking sheet. Top with pepper-onion mixture, ham, and cherry tomatoes. Sprinkle with shredded Swiss cheese. Bake in a 400° oven about 8 minutes or till cheese melts and pizza is heated through. Makes 4 servings.

Nutrition facts per serving: 529 calories, 21 g total fat (6 g saturated fat), 53 mg cholesterol, 1305 mg sodium, 57 g carbohydrate, 3 g fiber, 31 g protein. Daily Value: 12% vitamin A, 58% vitamin C, 33% calcium, 22% iron.

CURRIED FRUIT WITH HAM STEAK

A can of tropical fruit salad jump-starts the tangy, sweet sauce.

1   15¼-ounce can tropical fruit salad in
      light syrup or one 16-ounce can
      chunky mixed fruit in light syrup
1   1½-pound fully cooked center-cut
      ham slice, cut ¾-inch thick
1   small onion, chopped (⅓ cup)
½   to 1 teaspoon curry powder or
      ⅛ teaspoon ground nutmeg or
      ginger
1   tablespoon margarine or butter
2   teaspoons cornstarch
¼   cup pineapple juice or orange juice

Drain fruit, reserving syrup. Set aside. Trim separable fat from ham. Place ham on the *unheated* rack of a broiler pan. Broil 4 to 5 inches from the heat for 12 to 14 minutes or till heated through, turning once after half of the broiling time.

Meanwhile, for sauce, in a small saucepan cook onion and curry powder, nutmeg, or ginger in margarine or butter over medium heat till onion is tender. Stir in cornstarch. Add pineapple juice or orange juice and reserved fruit syrup. Cook and stir over medium heat till thickened and bubbly. Cook and stir for 2 minutes more. Carefully stir in drained fruit. Heat through. Serve warm sauce over ham. Makes 6 servings.

Nutrition facts per serving: 232 calories, 8 g total fat (2 g saturated fat), 60 mg cholesterol, 1390 mg sodium, 14 g carbohydrate, 1 g fiber, 24 g protein. Daily Value: 6% vitamin A, 46% vitamin C, 1% calcium, 13% iron.

HAM AND CHUTNEY PASTA SALAD

If you have some extra time before serving, quick-chill the ham mixture in the freezer for an additional 5 or 10 minutes.

  8 **ounces medium shell macaroni**
  ½ **cup chutney**
  ½ **cup mayonnaise or salad dressing**
  2 **green onions, sliced (¼ cup)**
  ⅛ **teaspoon coarsely ground pepper**
1½ **cups cubed fully cooked ham**
      (8 ounces)
  4 **lettuce leaves**
      Cherry tomato wedges (optional)

Cook macaroni according to package directions. Drain. Rinse with cold water. Drain again. Cover and place in the freezer while preparing chutney mixture.

Meanwhile, cut up any large pieces of the chutney. Stir together the chutney, mayonnaise or salad dressing, green onions, and pepper.

Toss together the chilled macaroni, chutney mixture, and ham. Line 4 salad plates with lettuce leaves. Serve ham mixture on lettuce-lined plates. Garnish with cherry tomatoes, if desired. Makes 4 servings.

Nutrition facts per serving: 580 calories, 26 g total fat (4 g saturated fat), 46 mg cholesterol, 850 mg sodium, 66 g carbohydrate, 2 g fiber, 20 g protein. Daily Value: 63% vitamin A, 25% vitamin C, 2% calcium, 23% iron.

FLORENTINE PIZZA

To use half a package of frozen spinach, micro-cook the unwrapped spinach on 30% power (medium-low) for 2 to 4 minutes or till soft enough to cut in half with a sharp knife. Rewrap one half and return to the freezer. Continue to cook the remaining half on 30% power for 3 to 5 minutes or till thawed.

½ pound bulk Italian sausage or bulk pork sausage
1 cup sliced fresh mushrooms
1 8-ounce can pizza sauce
½ of a 10-ounce package frozen chopped spinach, thawed and well drained
1 16-ounce package Boboli (12-inch Italian bread shell)
1 cup shredded mozzarella cheese (4 ounces)
Chili peppers (optional)

In a large skillet cook sausage and mushrooms till meat is no longer pink. Drain off fat. Pat meat mixture with paper towels to remove excess fat. Stir in pizza sauce and spinach. Cook and stir till heated through.

Meanwhile, place bread shell on a lightly greased baking sheet. Bake in a 400° oven for 5 minutes. Top with meat mixture. Sprinkle with shredded cheese. Bake for 8 to 10 minutes more or till cheese melts and pizza is heated through. Garnish with chili peppers, if desired. Makes 4 servings.

Nutrition facts per serving: 547 calories, 23 g total fat (7 g saturated fat), 54 mg cholesterol, 1483 mg sodium, 58 g carbohydrate, 2 g fiber, 30 g protein. Daily Value: 36% vitamin A, 30% vitamin C, 30% calcium, 24% iron.

MUSTARD-ORANGE LAMB CHOPS

You need only three ingredients for this delightful entrée.

8 lamb loin chops, cut ½-inch thick
3 tablespoons orange marmalade
4 teaspoons Dijon-style mustard

Trim separable fat from chops. Place chops on the *unheated* rack of a broiler pan. Broil 3 to 4 inches from the heat to desired doneness, turning once after half of the broiling time. (Allow 7 to 9 minutes for medium-rare to medium doneness.)

Meanwhile, in a small saucepan stir together the orange marmalade and mustard. Cook and stir over medium heat till heated through. Spoon over chops. Makes 4 servings.

Nutrition facts per serving: 228 calories, 9 g total fat (3 g saturated fat), 80 mg cholesterol, 199 mg sodium, 11 g carbohydrate, 1 g fiber, 26 g protein. Daily Value: 0% vitamin A, 1% vitamin C, 1% calcium, 11% iron.

GREEK-STYLE PASTA SKILLET
Lamb, cinnamon, and feta cheese add a Greek twist to this macaroni casserole.

¾   **pound ground lamb or ground beef**
1   **medium onion, chopped (½ cup)**
1   **14½-ounce can diced tomatoes**
1   **5½-ounce can tomato juice**
½   **cup water**
½   **teaspoon instant beef bouillon
      granules**
½   **teaspoon ground cinnamon**
⅛   **teaspoon garlic powder**
1   **cup medium shell macaroni or elbow
      macaroni**
1   **cup loose-pack frozen cut green beans**
½   **cup crumbled feta cheese**

In a large skillet cook ground lamb or beef and onion till meat is brown. Drain off fat. Stir in *undrained* tomatoes, tomato juice, water, bouillon granules, cinnamon, and garlic powder. Bring to boiling.

Stir uncooked macaroni and green beans into meat mixture. Return to boiling. Reduce heat. Cover and simmer about 15 minutes or till macaroni and green beans are tender. Sprinkle with feta cheese. Makes 4 servings.

Nutrition facts per serving: 362 calories, 16 g total fat (7 g saturated fat), 70 mg cholesterol, 647 mg sodium, 33 g carbohydrate, 2 g fiber, 22 g protein.
Daily Value: 12% vitamin A, 45% vitamin C, 12% calcium, 23% iron.

CHICKEN WITH HONEY-CRANBERRY SAUCE

A can of red cranberry sauce sweetened with honey and spiced with ginger makes a flavorful addition to quick-cooked chicken breasts.

4 large skinless, boneless chicken breast halves (1 pound total)
1 tablespoon margarine or butter
½ of a 16-ounce can (1 cup) whole cranberry sauce
2 tablespoons honey
½ teaspoon ground ginger

Rinse chicken; pat dry. In a large skillet cook chicken in hot margarine or butter over medium heat about 10 minutes or till no longer pink, turning once. Transfer chicken to a serving platter, reserving drippings in skillet. Keep chicken warm.

Stir cranberry sauce, honey, and ginger into the reserved drippings in the skillet. Cook and stir till heated through. Spoon over chicken. Makes 4 servings.

*Nutrition facts per serving: 284 calories, 6 g total fat (1 g saturated fat), 59 mg cholesterol, 108 mg sodium, 36 g carbohydrate, 1 g fiber, 22 g protein. **Daily Value:** 4% vitamin A, 4% vitamin C, 1% calcium, 6% iron.*

CUCUMBER CHICKEN PITA SANDWICHES
When it's too hot to cook, try this refreshing sandwich.

½ cup plain yogurt
¼ cup finely chopped cucumber
½ teaspoon dried dillweed
¼ teaspoon dried mint, crushed
4 large pita bread rounds
4 lettuce leaves
6 ounces thinly sliced fully cooked
     chicken breast
1 small tomato, thinly sliced
⅓ cup crumbled feta cheese

For dressing, in a small mixing bowl stir together yogurt, cucumber, dillweed, and mint. Set aside.

For each sandwich, place a pita bread round on a plate. Top with lettuce, chicken, tomato, and feta cheese. Spoon dressing on top. Roll up the pita bread. Secure with wooden toothpicks. Serve immediately. Makes 4 servings.

Nutrition facts per serving: 377 calories, 14 g total fat (5 g saturated fat), 55 mg cholesterol, 793 mg sodium, 43 g carbohydrate, 1 g fiber, 18 g protein. Daily Value: 6% vitamin A, 9% vitamin C, 19% calcium, 16% iron.

CHICKEN CURRY

Cooking the curry powder with the onion mellows the flavor yet retains the spiciness of this dish.

1½ cups quick-cooking rice
¾ pound skinless, boneless chicken
    breasts
2 tablespoons cooking oil
1 medium onion, chopped (½ cup)
1 to 2 teaspoons curry powder
3 tablespoons all-purpose flour
1 cup chicken broth
1 5½-ounce can tomato juice
1 11-ounce can mandarin orange
    sections, drained, or one 8-ounce
    can pineapple tidbits, drained
½ cup raisins, chopped cashews,
    chopped peanuts, coconut, and/or
    chopped banana
    Chives with flowers (optional)

Cook rice according to package directions. Meanwhile, rinse chicken; pat dry. Cut chicken into ¾-inch pieces.

In a large skillet heat *1 tablespoon* of the cooking oil over medium heat. Add chicken to hot oil; cook and stir for 2 to 3 minutes or till no longer pink. Remove chicken from the skillet, reserving drippings in skillet. Set chicken aside.

Add the remaining cooking oil to the reserved drippings. Cook the onion and curry powder in the oil-drippings mixture till onion is tender. Stir in flour. Stir in chicken broth and tomato juice. Cook and stir over medium heat till thickened and bubbly. Cook and stir for 1 minute more.

Return chicken to skillet. Gently stir in orange sections or pineapple. Cook till heated through. Serve over the hot cooked rice. Serve with raisins, cashews, peanuts, coconut, and/or banana. Garnish with fresh chives, if desired. Makes 4 servings.

Nutrition facts per serving: 423 calories, 10 g total fat (2 g saturated fat), 45 mg cholesterol, 385 mg sodium, 62 g carbohydrate, 2 g fiber, 22 g protein. ***Daily Value:*** *2% vitamin A, 14% vitamin C, 3% calcium, 21% iron.*

HOT CHICKEN-MUSTARD SALAD

A package of cleaned spinach is a great timesaver in this tangy salad. To save even more time, check your grocery store for chicken breasts cut into strips for stir-frying.

½ of a 1.1-ounce envelope
(2 tablespoons) honey-mustard
salad dressing mix
1 tablespoon cornstarch
Dash pepper
1 cup orange juice
8 cups packaged cleaned spinach or
mixed salad greens
1 medium carrot, thinly sliced (½ cup)
½ of a red or green sweet pepper, cut
into ¼-inch wide strips
¾ pound skinless, boneless chicken
breasts
1 tablespoon cooking oil

For sauce, in a small mixing bowl stir together salad dressing mix, cornstarch, and pepper. Gradually stir in orange juice. Set aside.

On 4 salad plates arrange spinach or mixed greens, carrot, and pepper strips. Set aside.

Rinse chicken; pat dry. Cut chicken into thin bite-size strips. In a large skillet cook and stir chicken in hot oil over medium heat for 2 to 3 minutes or till no longer pink. Remove chicken from skillet. Stir sauce mixture. Add to skillet. Cook and stir over medium heat till thickened and bubbly. Cook and stir for 2 minutes more. Return chicken to skillet. Heat through.

Spoon the chicken mixture over spinach or greens mixture on salad plates. Makes 4 servings.

Nutrition facts per serving: 204 calories, 6 g total fat (1 g saturated fat), 45 mg cholesterol, 371 mg sodium, 17 g carbohydrate, 4 g fiber, 20 g protein. ***Daily Value:*** *138% vitamin A, 136% vitamin C, 10% calcium, 25% iron.*

CHICKEN PICANTE

Keep this recipe in mind for days when you're really pressed for time. It's ready in 15 minutes, start to finish, and you only need three ingredients.

4   medium skinless, boneless chicken
      breast halves (12 ounces total)
¾   cup salsa
¼   cup apricot, peach, or pineapple
      preserves

Rinse chicken; pat dry. Place on the *unheated* rack of a broiler pan. Broil 4 to 5 inches from the heat for 10 to 12 minutes or till no longer pink, turning once after half of the broiling time.

Meanwhile, in a small saucepan stir together salsa and preserves. Cook and stir just till heated through and preserves are melted. Spoon over broiled chicken breast halves. Makes 4 servings.

Nutrition facts per serving: 160 calories, 3 g total fat (1 g saturated fat), 45 mg cholesterol, 209 mg sodium, 17 g carbohydrate, 0 g fiber, 17 g protein. ***Daily Value:*** *6% vitamin A, 23% vitamin C, 1% calcium, 7% iron.*

LEMON CHICKEN

Quick-cooking couscous is the perfect accompaniment for time-pressured cooks. Simply pour boiling water over the couscous; let it stand for 5 minutes. Fluff it with a fork and it's ready to eat.

4　large skinless, boneless chicken breast
　　halves (1 pound total)
⅓　cup all-purpose flour
¼　teaspoon pepper
2　tablespoons margarine or butter
1　cup chicken broth
¼　cup lemon juice
1　tablespoon cornstarch
2　green onions, sliced (¼ cup)
　　Hot cooked couscous (optional)
　　Lemon slices, cut in half (optional)

Rinse chicken; pat dry. Place each chicken breast between 2 pieces of plastic wrap. Working from the center to the edges, pound lightly with the flat side of a meat mallet till ¼-inch thick. In a shallow dish stir together flour and pepper. Lightly coat each piece of chicken with flour mixture.

In a large skillet cook chicken in hot margarine or butter over medium heat for 4 to 6 minutes or till no longer pink, turning once. Keep warm.

For sauce, in a small mixing bowl stir together chicken broth, lemon juice, and cornstarch. Add to skillet. Cook and stir over medium heat till thickened and bubbly. Cook and stir for 2 minutes more. Stir in green onions. Serve chicken with sauce, and, if desired, hot cooked couscous. Garnish with lemon slices, if desired. Makes 4 servings.

Nutrition facts per serving: 226 calories, 9 g total fat (2 g saturated fat), 60 mg cholesterol, 315 mg sodium, 10 g carbohydrate, 0 g fiber, 24 g protein. **Daily Value:** *8% vitamin A, 13% vitamin C, 1% calcium, 9% iron.*

MARGARITA CHICKEN

For soft, warm tortillas, wrap them in foil and heat in a 350° oven about 10 minutes. Or, micro-cook each unwrapped tortilla for 10 to 20 seconds on 100% power (high).

½ teaspoon finely shredded lime peel
¼ cup lime juice
2 tablespoons tequila
2 tablespoons honey
1 tablespoon cooking oil
2 teaspoons cornstarch
¼ teaspoon garlic salt
¼ teaspoon coarsely ground pepper
4 large skinless, boneless chicken breast halves (1 pound total)
4 flour tortillas, warmed
1 medium tomato, cut into 8 wedges
1 medium avocado, seeded, peeled, and cut up
  Lime slices, cut in half (optional)

For glaze, in a small saucepan stir together lime peel, lime juice, tequila, honey, cooking oil, cornstarch, garlic salt, and pepper. Cook and stir over medium heat till thickened and bubbly. Cook and stir for 2 minutes more.

Rinse chicken; pat dry. Place on the *unheated* rack of a broiler pan. Broil 4 to 5 inches from the heat for 12 to 15 minutes or till no longer pink, turning once after half of the broiling time and brushing with some of the glaze during the last 5 minutes.

Arrange chicken, warmed tortillas, tomato, and avocado on individual plates. Drizzle chicken with the remaining glaze. Garnish with lime slices, if desired. Makes 4 servings.

Nutrition facts per serving: 415 calories, 16 g total fat (3 g saturated fat), 59 mg cholesterol, 356 mg sodium, 39 g carbohydrate, 3 g fiber, 26 g protein. **Daily Value:** *7% vitamin A, 28% vitamin C, 5% calcium, 16% iron.*

ASPARAGUS-SAUCED CHICKEN

This recipe includes a quick-to-prepare white sauce mix, giving you plenty of flavor without all the fuss.

1½ cups quick-cooking rice
4   large skinless, boneless chicken breast halves or turkey breast tenderloin steaks (1 pound total)
1   cup milk
½   of a 1.8-ounce envelope (3 tablespoons) white sauce mix
2   tablespoons Dijon-style mustard
½   teaspoon instant chicken bouillon granules
½   of a 10-ounce package frozen cut asparagus or 1 cup loose-pack frozen cauliflower, broccoli and carrots

Prepare rice according to package directions.

Rinse chicken or turkey; pat dry. Place on the *unheated* rack of a broiler pan. Broil 4 to 5 inches from the heat for 12 to 15 minutes or till no longer pink, turning once after half of the broiling time.

Meanwhile, for sauce, in a small saucepan heat milk till warm. Stir in white sauce mix, mustard, and bouillon granules. Bring to boiling. Stir in asparagus or mixed vegetables. Return to boiling. Reduce heat. Cook and stir for 3 to 5 minutes more or till vegetables are crisp-tender. To serve, place chicken and rice on individual plates. Spoon sauce over all. Makes 4 servings.

Nutrition facts per serving: 334 calories, 7 g total fat (2 g saturated fat), 64 mg cholesterol, 602 mg sodium, 38 g carbohydrate, 1 g fiber, 28 g protein.
Daily Value: 7% vitamin A, 12% vitamin C, 11% calcium, 16% iron.

PLUM-SAUCED CHICKEN

Plum sauce mixed with a little vinegar gives a glistening glaze and a delightful sweet-and-sour flavor.

4　large skinless, boneless chicken breast
　　halves (1 pound total)
1　to 2 tablespoons margarine or butter
1　small onion, chopped (⅓ cup)
⅓　cup plum sauce
1　tablespoon vinegar
1　tablespoon water
¼　teaspoon five-spice powder
⅛　teaspoon garlic powder
　　Hot cooked fettuccine or spaghetti
　　(optional)

Rinse chicken; pat dry. In a large skillet cook chicken breast halves in *1 tablespoon* of the margarine or butter over medium heat about 10 minutes or till no longer pink, turning once. Remove chicken, reserving any drippings in skillet. Keep chicken warm.

For sauce, cook onion in reserved drippings till tender. (If necessary, add the additional 1 tablespoon margarine or butter to the skillet.) Stir in plum sauce, vinegar, water, five-spice powder, and garlic powder. Cook and stir till heated through. Serve chicken with sauce and, if desired, hot cooked fettuccine or spaghetti. Makes 4 servings.

Nutrition facts per serving: 182 calories, 6 g total fat (1 g saturated fat), 59 mg cholesterol, 94 mg sodium, 9 g carbohydrate, 0 g fiber, 22 g protein. **Daily Value:** *4% vitamin A, 3% vitamin C, 1% calcium, 5% iron.*

ORANGE-CHICKEN SALAD

An orange-scented sour cream dressing generously coats chicken strips, orange sections, and celery for a most refreshing main-dish salad.

⅓ cup dairy sour cream
⅓ cup mayonnaise or salad dressing
1 tablespoon frozen orange juice concentrate
½ teaspoon poppy seed (optional)
12 ounces sliced fully cooked chicken breast, cut into julienne strips
1 11-ounce can mandarin orange sections, drained, or one 15½-ounce can pineapple chunks, drained
3 stalks celery, cut into ½-inch slices (1½ cups)
2 green onions, sliced (¼ cup)
4 lettuce leaves

For dressing, in a small mixing bowl stir together sour cream, mayonnaise or salad dressing, orange juice concentrate, and, if desired, poppy seed.

In a large mixing bowl toss together the chicken strips, orange sections or pineapple chunks, celery, and green onions. Pour dressing over chicken mixture; toss lightly to coat. Season to taste with salt and pepper, if desired. Serve on lettuce leaves. Makes 4 servings.

Nutrition facts per serving: 378 calories, 23 g total fat (6 g saturated fat), 91 mg cholesterol, 250 mg sodium, 16 g carbohydrate, 2 g fiber, 28 g protein. Daily Value: 9% vitamin A, 21% vitamin C, 6% calcium, 10% iron.

SOUTHWEST CHICKEN SKILLET

Serve this family-pleasing, one-dish meal with corn muffins and a tossed salad.

¾ **pound skinless, boneless chicken breasts**
1 **tablespoon cooking oil**
1 **15-ounce jar salsa**
¾ **cup chicken broth**
½ **cup chopped green sweet pepper**
¼ **cup sliced pitted ripe olives (optional)**
1 **cup quick-cooking rice**
½ **cup shredded cheddar cheese or Monterey Jack cheese (2 ounces)**
   Green sweet pepper strips (optional)

Rinse chicken; pat dry. Cut chicken into 1-inch pieces.

In a large skillet cook and stir chicken in hot oil over medium heat for 2 to 3 minutes or till no longer pink.

Stir in salsa, chicken broth, chopped sweet pepper, and, if desired, olives. Bring to boiling. Stir in rice. Remove from heat. Sprinkle with cheese. Cover and let stand about 5 minutes or till rice is tender. Garnish with green pepper strips, if desired. Makes 4 servings.

Nutrition facts per serving: 344 calories, 15 g total fat (4 g saturated fat), 60 mg cholesterol, 1012 mg sodium, 34 g carbohydrate, 0 g fiber, 25 g protein. Daily Value: 37% vitamin A, 126% vitamin C, 12% calcium, 24% iron.

EASY SWEET-AND-SOUR CHICKEN

Skip the hassle of deep-frying chicken pieces—use this recipe and start with frozen chicken chunks instead.

1   **10-ounce package frozen breaded
      fully cooked chicken chunks**
1½ **cups quick-cooking rice**
1   **8-ounce can pineapple tidbits
      (juice pack)**
1   **large red or green sweet pepper,
      cut into 1-inch pieces**
¼   **cup red wine vinegar or vinegar**
3   **tablespoons sugar**
2   **tablespoons cornstarch**
2   **tablespoons soy sauce**
½   **teaspoon instant chicken bouillon
      granules**
1   **8-ounce can sliced water chestnuts,
      drained**
      Parsley sprigs (optional)

Bake frozen chicken chunks according to package directions. Prepare quick-cooking rice according to package directions.

Meanwhile, drain pineapple, reserving juice. Add enough water to reserved juice to equal 1½ cups. Pour pineapple juice mixture into a medium saucepan. Add sweet red or green pepper. Bring to boiling. Reduce heat. Cover and simmer for 1 to 2 minutes or till pepper is crisp-tender.

Stir together vinegar, sugar, cornstarch, soy sauce, and chicken bouillon granules. Stir into mixture in the saucepan. Cook and stir over medium heat till thickened and bubbly. Cook and stir for 2 minutes more. Gently stir in chicken chunks, pineapple tidbits, and water chestnuts. Heat through. Serve chicken mixture over hot cooked rice. Garnish with parsley sprigs, if desired. Makes 4 servings.

Nutrition facts per serving: 434 calories, 10 g total fat (1 g saturated fat), 67 mg cholesterol, 1142 mg sodium, 68 g carbohydrate, 1 g fiber, 19 g protein.
***Daily Value:** 20% vitamin A, 81% vitamin C, 2% calcium, 22% iron.*

SOUTHWEST CHICKEN SOUP

Use your choice of mild, medium, or hot salsa to gauge the spiciness of this soup.

½ **pound skinless, boneless chicken
      breasts**
1 **tablespoon cooking oil**
2 **14½-ounce cans chicken broth**
1 **16-ounce jar salsa**
1 **cup frozen loose-pack whole
      kernel corn**
   Tortilla chips (optional)

Rinse chicken; pat dry. Cut chicken into ¾-inch pieces. In a large saucepan cook and stir chicken in hot oil over medium heat for 2 to 3 minutes or till no longer pink. Remove chicken from saucepan. Drain oil from saucepan.

In the same saucepan stir together chicken broth, salsa, and corn. Bring to boiling. Reduce heat. Cover and simmer for 5 to 6 minutes or till corn is tender. Stir in chicken. Heat through. Ladle into soup bowls. Serve with tortilla chips, if desired. Makes 4 servings.

Nutrition facts per serving: 263 calories, 14 g total fat (4 g saturated fat), 46 mg cholesterol, 1556 mg sodium, 23 g carbohydrate, 0 g fiber, 22 g protein. Daily Value: 33% vitamin A, 110% vitamin C, 12% calcium, 20% iron.

MOLASSES-ORANGE GLAZED CHICKEN

This easy glaze gives the chicken a golden color and a sweet-citrus flavor.

2   tablespoons frozen orange juice
       concentrate, thawed
2   tablespoons molasses
¼   teaspoon onion powder
4   medium skinless, boneless chicken
       breast halves (12 ounces total)
       or 8 small skinless, boneless
       chicken thighs
       Hot cooked spinach fettuccine or
       plain fettuccine (optional)
       Orange peel strips (optional)

For glaze, in a small mixing bowl stir together orange juice concentrate, molasses, and onion powder.

Rinse chicken; pat dry. Season with salt and pepper. Place on the *unheated* rack of a broiler pan. Broil 4 to 5 inches from the heat for 5 minutes. Brush with some of the glaze. Turn chicken and brush with remaining glaze. Broil for 5 to 9 minutes more or till chicken is no longer pink. If desired, serve with fettuccine and garnish with orange peel strips. Makes 4 servings.

Nutrition facts per serving: 160 calories, 3 g total fat (1 g saturated fat), 59 mg cholesterol, 56 mg sodium, 10 g carbohydrate, 0 g fiber, 22 g protein. **Daily Value:** *0% vitamin A, 22% vitamin C, 2% calcium, 8% iron.*

TURKEY PARMIGIANA

Can't find turkey tenderloin steaks? Just buy 2 whole turkey tenderloins and horizontally cut each in half to make 4 steaks.

8 ounces spaghetti
4 turkey breast tenderloin steaks
    (1 pound total)
1 tablespoon margarine or butter
2 tablespoons grated Parmesan cheese
1 14-ounce jar tomato and herb
    pasta sauce
¾ cup shredded mozzarella cheese
    (3 ounces)

Cook spaghetti according to package directions. Drain.

Meanwhile, rinse turkey; pat dry. In a large skillet cook turkey in hot margarine or butter over medium heat for 10 to 12 minutes or till no longer pink, turning once. Sprinkle turkey with Parmesan cheese. Spoon pasta sauce over turkey. Cover and cook for 1 to 2 minutes or till heated through.

Sprinkle turkey with mozzarella cheese. Cover and let stand for 1 to 2 minutes or till cheese is melted. Serve with hot cooked spaghetti. Makes 4 servings.

*Nutrition facts per serving: 518 calories, 12 g total fat (4 g saturated fat), 64 mg cholesterol, 561 mg sodium, 62 g carbohydrate, 0 g fiber, 37 g protein. **Daily Value:** 25% vitamin A, 30% vitamin C, 20% calcium, 28% iron.*

MUSTARD-GLAZED TURKEY BURGERS

Here's a new burger for your family to try. Serve it with baked beans and potato chips.

2   tablespoons Dijon-style mustard
      or brown mustard
1   tablespoon corn syrup
1   beaten egg
¼   cup fine dry bread crumbs
¼   teaspoon salt
¼   teaspoon dried sage, crushed
⅛   teaspoon pepper
1   pound ground raw turkey or ground
      raw chicken
1   tablespoon margarine or butter
1   15½-ounce can pineapple slices,
      drained
6   hamburger buns, split and toasted
      Shredded lettuce

For glaze, in a small mixing bowl stir together mustard and corn syrup. Set aside.

In a medium mixing bowl stir together egg, bread crumbs, salt, sage, and pepper. Add ground turkey or chicken. Mix well. Shape into six ½-inch-thick patties.

In a large skillet cook patties in hot margarine or butter over medium heat for 10 to 12 minutes or till no longer pink, turning once. Top each patty with a pineapple slice. (Reserve remaining pineapple slices for another use.) Spoon glaze over patties during the last 1 minute of cooking. Place lettuce on bun bottoms. Top with patties and bun tops. Makes 6 servings.

Nutrition facts per serving: 318 calories, 11 g total fat (3 g saturated fat), 64 mg cholesterol, 518 mg sodium, 39 g carbohydrate, 1 g fiber, 15 g protein. Daily Value: 4% vitamin A, 11% vitamin C, 5% calcium, 16% iron.

TURKEY SAUSAGE AND BEAN SOUP

This soup tastes like it simmered all day even though it can be ready in less than 20 minutes. The secret is the smoky flavor of the turkey kielbasa.

4 cups chicken broth
2 15-ounce cans white kidney beans
     (cannellini), great northern beans,
     or red kidney beans, rinsed
     and drained
8 ounces fully cooked turkey kielbasa,
     cut into bite-size pieces
1 medium onion, chopped (½ cup)
1 teaspoon dried basil, crushed
¼ teaspoon coarsely ground pepper
1 clove garlic, minced, or ⅛ teaspoon
     garlic powder
3 cups packaged, cleaned spinach

In a Dutch oven or large saucepan combine chicken broth, beans, sausage, onion, basil, pepper, and garlic or garlic powder. Bring to boiling. Reduce heat. Cover and simmer for 10 to 15 minutes or till onion is tender.

Meanwhile, remove stems from spinach. Stack the leaves one on top of the other and cut into 1-inch-wide strips. Just before serving, stir spinach into soup. Makes 4 servings.

Nutrition facts per serving: 257 calories, 6 g total fat (2 g saturated fat), 39 mg cholesterol, 1620 mg sodium, 35 g carbohydrate, 11 g fiber, 28 g protein. Daily Value: 19% vitamin A, 16% vitamin C, 9% calcium, 31% iron.

PARMESAN-TURKEY SANDWICHES

Keep the ingredients on hand for this hearty sandwich, and you'll be prepared for the next time your teenager invites friends over for dinner and forgets to tell you.

½ cup cornflake crumbs or crushed rich
    round crackers (about 12)
¼ cup grated Parmesan cheese
⅛ teaspoon garlic powder
⅛ teaspoon pepper
1 beaten egg
1 tablespoon water
4 turkey breast tenderloin steaks
    (1 pound total)
2 tablespoons margarine or butter
4 lettuce leaves
4 hoagie buns, split and toasted
¼ cup creamy Parmesan or creamy
    buttermilk ranch salad dressing
2 tomatoes, thinly sliced

In a shallow dish stir together cornflake crumbs or crushed crackers, Parmesan cheese, garlic powder, and pepper. In another shallow dish beat together egg and water. Dip turkey steaks into egg mixture. Coat with crumbs.

In a large skillet cook turkey in hot margarine or butter over medium heat for 8 to 10 minutes or till no longer pink, turning once.

Place lettuce on bottom halves of hoagie buns. Top with turkey, salad dressing, and tomato slices. Add bun tops. Makes 4 servings.

Nutrition facts per serving: 686 calories, 21 g total fat (5 g saturated fat), 112 mg cholesterol, 1177 mg sodium, 83 g carbohydrate, 5 g fiber, 39 g protein. Daily Value: 22% vitamin A, 16% vitamin C, 14% calcium, 32% iron.

HERBED TURKEY AND BROCCOLI

Soft-style cream cheese makes an ultra-rich sauce for this one-pan pasta dish.

2 quarts water
8 ounces linguine or spaghetti, broken
    in half
3 cups small broccoli flowerets
1 8-ounce container soft-style cream
    cheese with garlic and herbs
⅔ cup milk
¼ teaspoon coarsely ground pepper
6 ounces sliced fully cooked
    smoked turkey breast, cut into
    bite-size strips

In a Dutch oven bring water to boiling. Add linguine or spaghetti a little at a time. Return to boiling. Reduce heat. Cook for 6 minutes. Add broccoli. Return to boiling. Cook for 2 to 3 minutes more or till pasta is tender and broccoli is crisp-tender. Drain.

In the same Dutch oven combine cream cheese, milk, and pepper. Cook and stir over low heat till cream cheese is melted. Add pasta-broccoli mixture and turkey. Toss till coated with the cheese mixture. If necessary, stir in additional milk to make desired consistency. Makes 4 servings.

Nutrition facts per serving: 516 calories, 21 g total fat (11 g saturated fat), 81 mg cholesterol, 675 mg sodium, 57 g carbohydrate, 4 g fiber, 25 g protein. Daily Value: 29% vitamin A, 126% vitamin C, 11% calcium, 23% iron.

HOT TURKEY SUB SANDWICH

Pair this hefty sandwich with bowls of tomato soup.

1 tablespoon olive oil
1 teaspoon dried basil, crushed
1 clove garlic, minced, or ⅛ teaspoon
    garlic powder
1 8-ounce loaf or ½ of a 16-ounce loaf
    unsliced French bread
6 ounces sliced mozzarella cheese
4 ounces sliced fully cooked
    smoked turkey
2 tablespoons sliced pitted ripe olives
2 tomatoes, thinly sliced
⅛ teaspoon coarsely ground black
    pepper

In a small mixing bowl stir together the olive oil, basil, and garlic or garlic powder. Split the French bread lengthwise. Use a spoon to hollow out the top half, leaving a ¾-inch shell. Brush the cut sides of both halves with the olive oil mixture.

On the bottom half of the French bread, layer *half* of the mozzarella cheese, all of the smoked turkey, the olives, the remaining cheese, and the tomato slices. Sprinkle with pepper. Top with the bread top. Wrap in heavy duty foil.

Bake in a 375° oven about 10 minutes or till heated through. Cut into 4 portions. Makes 4 servings.

*Nutrition facts per serving: 335 calories, 13 g total fat (5 g saturated fat), 36 mg cholesterol, 849 mg sodium, 33 g carbohydrate, 1 g fiber, 22 g protein. **Daily Value:** 9% vitamin A, 10% vitamin C, 27% calcium, 13% iron.*

SAUSAGE-VEGETABLE SOUP

For a Louisiana spin on this hearty soup, try Cajun-style stewed tomatoes and add a couple dashes of bottled hot pepper sauce.

1   14½-ounce can beef broth
1   14½-ounce can diced tomatoes with Italian herbs or Italian-style stewed tomatoes, cut up
1½ cups water
2   cups frozen loose-pack diced hash brown potatoes
1   10-ounce package frozen mixed vegetables
8   ounces fully cooked smoked turkey sausage, halved lengthwise and cut into ½-inch pieces
⅛   teaspoon pepper
2   tablespoons grated Parmesan cheese (optional)

In a large saucepan combine beef broth, *undrained* tomatoes, and water. Bring to boiling. Stir in hash brown potatoes, mixed vegetables, sausage, and pepper. Return to boiling. Reduce heat. Cover and simmer for 5 to 10 minutes or till vegetables are tender.

Ladle into soup bowls. Sprinkle with Parmesan cheese, if desired. Makes 4 servings.

Nutrition facts per serving: 257 calories, 9 g total fat (3 g saturated fat), 36 mg cholesterol, 1202 mg sodium, 29 g carbohydrate, 1 g fiber, 16 g protein. Daily Value: 37% vitamin A, 27% vitamin C, 7% calcium, 17% iron.

SPICY FILLETS WITH TOASTED PECANS

The crispy coating and toasted pecans earmark this pan-fried fish as a sample of Southern-style cooking.

¼ cup all-purpose flour
2 tablespoons yellow cornmeal
1 teaspoon chili powder
½ teaspoon garlic salt
1 pound fresh firm-textured fish fillets,
   ½ to 1 inch thick (such as catfish,
   pike, lake trout, or orange roughy)
3 tablespoons margarine or butter
¼ cup broken pecans
1 tablespoon lemon juice
⅛ teaspoon ground red pepper

In a shallow dish stir together flour, cornmeal, chili powder, and garlic salt. Dip fish into flour mixture.

In a 12-inch skillet cook fish in *2 tablespoons* of the margarine or butter over medium heat for 4 to 10 minutes or till fish flakes easily and coating is golden, turning once. Remove fish from skillet; keep warm.

Melt the remaining 1 tablespoon margarine or butter in the skillet. Add pecans; cook and stir over medium heat for 3 to 5 minutes or till lightly toasted. Stir in lemon juice and red pepper. Drizzle pecan mixture over fish fillets. Makes 4 servings.

Nutrition facts per serving: 267 calories, 14 g total fat (2 g saturated fat), 45 mg cholesterol, 407 mg sodium, 11 g carbohydrate, 1 g fiber, 24 g protein. **Daily Value:** *15% vitamin A, 9% vitamin C, 6% calcium, 9% iron.*

HERB-BUTTERED FISH STEAKS

If you can't find small fish fillets, buy two large ones and cut them in half before serving. If the fillets are 1-inch thick, the cooking time will be the same.

2   tablespoons butter or margarine,
       softened
1   teaspoon finely shredded lime peel
       or lemon peel
1   teaspoon lime juice or lemon juice
1   teaspoon snipped fresh tarragon or
       rosemary or ¼ teaspoon dried
       tarragon or rosemary, crushed
4   small or 2 large halibut, salmon,
       shark, or swordfish steaks, cut
       1-inch thick (about 1 pound total)
1   teaspoon butter or margarine, melted
    Lime or lemon slices, cut in half
       (optional)
    Fresh tarragon or rosemary (optional)

For the herb butter, in a small mixing bowl stir together the 2 tablespoons butter or margarine, lime or lemon peel, lime or lemon juice, and tarragon or rosemary. Set aside.

Place the fish steaks on the lightly greased rack of a broiler pan. Brush with the 1 teaspoon melted butter or margarine. Broil 4 to 5 inches from the heat for 8 to 12 minutes or till fish flakes easily, turning once after half of the broiling time. To serve, top each serving with one-fourth of the herb butter. Garnish with lime or lemon slices and fresh tarragon or rosemary, if desired. Makes 4 servings.

Nutrition facts per serving: 184 calories, 9 g total fat (2 g saturated fat), 36 mg cholesterol, 140 mg sodium, 0 g carbohydrate, 0 g fiber, 24 g protein. Daily Value: 12% vitamin A, 1% vitamin C, 4% calcium, 6% iron.

OVEN-FRIED FISH

Individually frozen fish fillets are perfect for busy cooks because you can cook them without thawing them first. In this easy recipe we toss them in seasoned crumbs and bake them in the oven.

2 **tablespoons margarine or butter**
¾ **cup cornflake crumbs**
¾ **teaspoon onion salt**
¼ **teaspoon pepper**
1 **beaten egg**
1 **tablespoon water**
1 **pound individually frozen fish fillets**
    Tartar sauce (optional)

Preheat oven to 450°. Place margarine or butter in a shallow baking pan. Place the pan in the oven for 2 to 3 minutes or till margarine or butter melts.

In a shallow dish stir together the cornflake crumbs, onion salt, and pepper. In another shallow dish combine beaten egg and water. Measure thickness of fish. Dip frozen fish fillets into egg mixture. Coat with crumb mixture. Place in the baking pan on top of the melted margarine or butter.

Bake, uncovered, in the 450° oven till fish flakes easily. (Allow 9 to 11 minutes per ½-inch thickness of fish.) Serve with tartar sauce, if desired. Makes 4 servings.

Nutrition facts per serving: 175 calories, 8 g total fat (2 g saturated fat), 96 mg cholesterol, 414 mg sodium, 5 g carbohydrate, 0 g fiber, 20 g protein. **Daily Value:** *18% vitamin A, 6% vitamin C, 1% calcium, 6% iron.*

ORIENTAL-GLAZED TUNA STEAKS

Look for an Oriental-style rice mix to serve with these zesty steaks.

1 **pound fresh tuna or swordfish steaks,
    cut ½-inch thick**
⅔ **cup orange juice**
2 **tablespoons soy sauce**
1 **teaspoon toasted sesame oil**
1 **teaspoon grated gingerroot**
¼ **teaspoon bottled minced garlic**

Cut fish into 4 serving-size pieces, if necessary. Place fish in a plastic bag. For marinade, stir together orange juice, soy sauce, sesame oil, gingerroot, and garlic. Pour over fish. Let stand at room temperature for 10 minutes. Drain fish, reserving marinade.

Place fish on lightly greased rack of a broiler pan. Broil 4 to 5 inches from the heat for 4 to 6 minutes or till fish flakes easily with a fork.

Meanwhile, pour reserved marinade into a small saucepan. Bring to boiling. Boil for 3 to 4 minutes or till reduced by half, stirring frequently. Drizzle cooked marinade over fish steaks. Makes 4 servings.

Nutrition facts per serving: 211 calories, 7 g total fat (2 g saturated fat), 47 mg cholesterol, 563 mg sodium, 5 g carbohydrate, 0 g fiber, 30 g protein. Daily Value: 73% vitamin A, 34% vitamin C, 1% calcium, 10% iron.

VEGETABLE-TOPPED FISH
Salsa and summer squash make an easy sauce for baked fillets.

1   pound fresh fish fillets
2   teaspoons margarine or butter, melted
⅛   teaspoon salt
⅛   teaspoon pepper
1   8-ounce jar salsa (about 1 cup)
1   small yellow summer squash or
      zucchini, halved lengthwise and
      cut into ¼-inch thick slices

Measure thickness of fish. Place the fish in a greased shallow baking pan, turning under any thin portions. Brush fish with melted margarine or butter. Sprinkle with salt and pepper. Bake, uncovered, in a 450° oven till fish flakes easily. (Allow 4 to 6 minutes per ½-inch thickness of fish.)

Meanwhile, in a small saucepan stir together salsa and summer squash or zucchini. Bring to boiling. Reduce heat. Cover and simmer for 5 to 6 minutes or till squash is crisp-tender. Serve squash mixture over baked fish fillets. Makes 4 servings.

Nutrition facts per serving: 202 calories, 10 g total fat (2 g saturated fat), 44 mg cholesterol, 638 mg sodium, 13 g carbohydrate, 1 g fiber, 19 g protein. Daily Value: 20% vitamin A, 59% vitamin C, 4% calcium, 14% iron.

FISH SANDWICHES

Try these easy and economical sandwiches for a Saturday lunch.

4   frozen crumb-coated fish fillets or
        patties (10 to 12 ounces total)
4   thin tomato slices
½   teaspoon dried basil, crushed
⅛   teaspoon pepper
4   ounces mozzarella, cheddar, Swiss,
        or American cheese, thinly sliced
2   tablespoons buttermilk ranch, creamy
        cucumber, or creamy Parmesan
        salad dressing
4   hamburger buns, split and toasted

Bake fish fillets or patties according to package directions.

Top each fillet or pattie with a tomato slice. Sprinkle each with basil and pepper. Top each with cheese. Return to the oven for 2 to 3 minutes or till cheese is melted.

Spread the salad dressing over the bottom halves of the buns. Top with fish and bun tops. Makes 4 servings.

Nutrition facts per serving: 444 calories, 20 g total fat (6 g saturated fat), 108 mg cholesterol, 854 mg sodium, 43 g carbohydrate, 3 g fiber, 23 g protein. ***Daily Value:*** *10% vitamin A, 10% vitamin C, 19% calcium, 12% iron.*

MUSTARD-TOPPED SALMON

Delicious on salmon, the mustard topping also perks up any broiled fish such as orange roughy, red snapper, cod, or halibut.

1 **pound fresh salmon fillets**
2 **tablespoons mayonnaise, salad dressing, dairy sour cream, or plain yogurt**
1 **tablespoon Dijon-style mustard**
1 **teaspoon lemon-pepper seasoning**

Measure thickness of fish. Cut fish into serving-size pieces. Place fish, skin side down, on the lightly greased rack of a broiler pan, turning under any thin portions of the fillets. Broil 4 to 5 inches from the heat till nearly done. (Allow 4 minutes for each ½-inch thickness.)

Meanwhile, in a small mixing bowl stir together mayonnaise, salad dressing, sour cream, or yogurt; Dijon-style mustard; and lemon-pepper seasoning. Spread mustard mixture over the fish. Broil for 1 to 2 minutes more or till fish flakes easily and mustard mixture is lightly browned. Makes 4 servings.

Nutrition facts per serving: 159 calories, 10 g total fat (2 g saturated fat), 24 mg cholesterol, 473 mg sodium, 1 g carbohydrate, 0 g fiber, 17 g protein. Daily Value: 2% vitamin A, 0% vitamin C, 1% calcium, 5% iron.

HOT TUNA HOAGIES

This may be a sandwich, but you'll need a knife and fork to eat it.

1½   cups packaged shredded cabbage
      with carrot (coleslaw mix)
 1   9¼-ounce can tuna (water pack),
      drained and broken into chunks
 2   tablespoons mayonnaise or
      salad dressing
 2   tablespoons buttermilk ranch, creamy
      cucumber, or creamy Parmesan
      salad dressing
 2   hoagie buns, split and toasted
 2   ounces cheddar cheese or Swiss
      cheese, thinly sliced

In a medium mixing bowl toss together shredded cabbage with carrot and tuna. In a small mixing bowl stir together mayonnaise or salad dressing and ranch, cucumber, or Parmesan salad dressing. Toss salad dressing mixture with tuna mixture.

Spread tuna mixture evenly on the four halves of the hoagie buns. Place on the *unheated* rack of a broiler pan. Broil 4 to 5 inches from the heat for 2 to 3 minutes or till heated through. Top with cheese. Broil 30 to 60 seconds more or till cheese melts. Makes 4 servings.

Nutrition facts per serving: 417 calories, 16 g total fat (5 g saturated fat), 40 mg cholesterol, 788 mg sodium, 41 g carbohydrate, 3 g fiber, 27 g protein. **Daily Value:** *26% vitamin A, 19% vitamin C, 13% calcium, 19% iron.*

EASY SALMON PASTA

To save time, we cook the pasta and vegetables together in the same pan.

2   cups frozen loose-pack mixed
        vegetables or one 10-ounce package
        frozen mixed vegetables
1½ cups corkscrew macaroni (rotini)
2   green onions, sliced (¼ cup)
1   10¾-ounce can condensed cheddar
        cheese soup
½   cup milk
½   teaspoon dried dillweed
¼   teaspoon dry mustard
⅛   teaspoon pepper
2   6¾-ounce cans skinless, boneless
        salmon or two 6½-ounce cans
        tuna, drained
    Fresh dill (optional)

In a large saucepan cook frozen vegetables, pasta, and green onions in boiling water for 10 to 12 minutes or till pasta is just tender. Drain.

Stir soup, milk, dillweed, dry mustard, and pepper into pasta mixture. Gently fold in salmon or tuna. Cook over low heat till heated through. Garnish with fresh dill, if desired. Makes 5 servings.

Nutrition facts per serving: 347 calories, 9 g total fat (4 g saturated fat), 56 mg cholesterol, 827 mg sodium, 41 g carbohydrate, 1 g fiber, 22 g protein.
Daily Value: *35% vitamin A, 4% vitamin C, 10% calcium, 20% iron.*

SHRIMP IN GARLIC SAUCE

Stir-fry the shrimp just till they turn pink. Overcooking toughens them.

1½ cups water
¼ teaspoon salt
1½ cups quick-cooking rice
½ cup chicken broth
1½ teaspoons cornstarch
1 medium red sweet pepper, cut into
    thin strips
1 medium green sweet pepper, cut into
    thin strips
1 small onion, cut into thin wedges
2 to 3 teaspoons bottled minced garlic
1 tablespoon margarine or butter
1 12-ounce package frozen, peeled,
    deveined shrimp, thawed
1 tablespoon margarine or butter
2 tablespoons snipped fresh parsley

In a medium saucepan bring water and salt to boiling. Stir in rice. Cover; remove from heat. Let stand till serving time. For sauce, stir together chicken broth and cornstarch. Set aside.

In a wok or large skillet cook red pepper, green pepper, onion, and garlic in 1 tablespoon margarine or butter over medium-high heat about 3 minutes or till pepper and onion are crisp-tender. Remove vegetables from the wok. Add shrimp and 1 tablespoon margarine or butter. Stir-fry over medium-high heat for 3 to 4 minutes or till shrimp turn pink.

Push shrimp from the center of the wok. Stir sauce; add to the center of the wok. Cook and stir till thickened and bubbly. Return vegetables to the wok. Stir ingredients together to coat with sauce. Cook and stir about 1 minute more or till heated through.

Stir parsley into rice. Immediately serve shrimp mixture over hot rice. Makes 4 servings.

Nutrition facts per serving: 285 calories, 7 g total fat (1 g saturated fat), 131 mg cholesterol, 453 mg sodium, 37 g carbohydrate, 1 g fiber, 18 g protein. ***Daily Value:*** *27% vitamin A, 81% vitamin C, 4% calcium, 25% iron.*

NO-CHOP SCALLOP STIR-FRY

Scallops are available in two sizes. Bay scallops measure about ½ inch in diameter and sea scallops about 1½ inches. Both are delicious in this easy stir-fry dish, but cut the large scallops in half before cooking.

6	cups water
8	ounces Chinese egg noodles or vermicelli, broken into 3- to 4-inch pieces
¼	cup soy sauce
3	tablespoons dry sherry or apple juice
½	teaspoon ground ginger
12	ounces fresh bay or sea scallops
1	tablespoon cooking oil
1½	teaspoons bottled minced garlic
2	cups loose-pack frozen stir-fry vegetables

In a large saucepan bring water to boiling. Cook egg noodles or vermicelli in boiling water till al dente. (Allow 3 to 4 minutes for egg noodles or 5 to 7 minutes for vermicelli.) Drain. Rinse and drain again; set aside.

Meanwhile, for sauce, stir together soy sauce, sherry or apple juice, and ginger; set aside. Cut any large scallops in half; set aside.

Pour cooking oil into a wok or large skillet. (Add more oil as necessary during cooking.) Preheat over medium-high heat. Stir-fry garlic in hot oil for 15 seconds. Add frozen vegetables. Stir-fry for 2 to 3 minutes or till crisp-tender. Remove the vegetables from the wok.

Add the scallops to the hot wok. Stir-fry for 2 to 3 minutes or till opaque. Push scallops from the center of the wok. Stir sauce. Add sauce to the center of the wok. Return vegetables to the wok. Add noodles to the wok. Toss all of the ingredients together to coat with sauce. Serve immediately. Makes 4 servings.

Nutrition facts per serving: 285 calories, 6 g total fat (1 g saturated fat), 62 mg cholesterol, 1178 mg sodium, 37 g carbohydrate, 0 g fiber, 18 g protein. **Daily Value:** *50% vitamin A, 36% vitamin C, 7% calcium, 24% iron.*

CRAB AND FRUIT SALAD

Store the can of mandarin orange sections in the refrigerator and they will be icy cold when you are ready to add them to the salad.

½ cup mayonnaise or salad dressing
1 green onion, sliced (2 tablespoons)
1 tablespoon frozen orange juice concentrate, thawed
½ teaspoon ground ginger
 Dash ground red pepper
8 ounces lump crabmeat or one 8-ounce package frozen crab-flavored, flake-style fish, thawed
6 cups torn mixed salad greens
2 cups strawberries, halved
1 11-ounce can mandarin orange sections, drained
¼ cup pecan pieces (optional)

In a medium mixing bowl stir together mayonnaise or salad dressing, green onion, orange juice concentrate, ginger, and red pepper. Gently stir in crab meat or crab-flavored fish. Cover and chill in the freezer about 10 minutes or till cold.

Meanwhile, toss together mixed greens, strawberries, and orange sections. Arrange on four salad plates. Divide the crab mixture among the salad plates. Sprinkle with pecans, if desired. Makes 4 servings.

Nutrition facts per serving: 334 calories, 24 g total fat (3 g saturated fat), 73 mg cholesterol, 358 mg sodium, 19 g carbohydrate, 3 g fiber, 14 g protein. *Daily Value:* 33% vitamin A, 104% vitamin C, 10% calcium, 16% iron.

SHRIMP AND PLUM TOMATOES WITH PASTA

Plum tomatoes and tarragon impart a garden fresh flavor to this delightful combination.

1   12-ounce package frozen, peeled, and
    deveined shrimp
1   9-ounce package refrigerated spinach
    or plain fettuccine
1   medium onion, chopped (½ cup)
1   teaspoon bottled minced garlic
1   tablespoon olive oil or cooking oil
4   medium plum tomatoes, chopped
    (about 1⅔ cups)
2   teaspoons snipped fresh tarragon or
    ½ teaspoon dried tarragon, crushed
¼   teaspoon coarsely ground pepper

In a large saucepan cook the shrimp with the fettuccine according to fettuccine package directions. Drain. Return to the hot saucepan.

Meanwhile, in a medium saucepan cook onion and garlic in hot oil till onion is tender. Stir in tomatoes, tarragon, and pepper. Cook over low heat, stirring occasionally, for 2 to 3 minutes or till hot.

Add tomato mixture to fettuccine mixture in saucepan. Toss to mix. Makes 4 servings.

Nutrition facts per serving: 277 calories, 5 g total fat (1 g saturated fat), 131 mg cholesterol, 173 mg sodium, 37 g carbohydrate, 1 g fiber, 20 g protein. Daily Value: 11% vitamin A, 25% vitamin C, 6% calcium, 24% iron.

VEGGIE SKILLET

For a Mexican version, use 1 cup tomato sauce and 1 cup salsa in place of the spaghetti sauce.

3 cups frozen loose-pack diced hash
   brown potatoes with onion
   and peppers
2 tablespoons cooking oil
2 cups meatless spaghetti sauce
   with mushrooms or Italian
   cooking sauce
1 cup loose-pack frozen peas and carrots
1 cup loose-pack frozen whole
   kernel corn
½ cup shredded cheddar cheese or
   mozzarella cheese (2 ounces)

In a large skillet cook potatoes in hot oil over medium heat for 6 to 8 minutes or till nearly tender, stirring occasionally.

Stir spaghetti sauce or Italian cooking sauce, peas and carrots, and corn into the potatoes in the skillet. Bring to boiling. Reduce heat. Cover and simmer for 5 to 7 minutes or till vegetables are tender. Sprinkle with cheese. Let stand, covered, about 1 minute or till cheese is melted. Makes 4 servings.

Nutrition facts per serving: 406 calories, 21 g total fat (6 g saturated fat), 20 mg cholesterol, 742 mg sodium, 49 g carbohydrate, 5 g fiber, 10 g protein. **Daily Value:** *50% vitamin A, 45% vitamin C, 12% calcium, 14% iron.*

PASTA WITH THREE CHEESES

Cream cheese, Parmesan cheese, and your choice of Gouda, Edam, havarti, fontina, cheddar, or Swiss cheese make up the flavor-rich sauce.

10 ounces medium shell or corkscrew macaroni (rotini)
 2 cups loose-pack frozen cauliflower, broccoli, and carrots or other vegetable combination
 1 cup milk
 1 3-ounce package cream cheese, cut up
 ¼ teaspoon coarsely ground pepper
 ¾ cup shredded Gouda, Edam, havarti, fontina, cheddar, or Swiss cheese (3 ounces)
 ¼ cup grated Parmesan cheese
   Grated Parmesan cheese (optional)

In a large saucepan cook shell or corkscrew macaroni according to package directions, *except* add the frozen vegetables during the last 5 minutes of cooking. Drain.

In the hot saucepan combine milk, cream cheese, and pepper. Cook and stir over low heat till cheese is melted.

Return macaroni mixture to saucepan. Toss to coat with milk mixture. Gently stir in the shredded cheese and the ¼ cup Parmesan cheese. Transfer to a serving bowl. Sprinkle with additional Parmesan cheese, if desired. Makes 4 servings.

Nutrition facts per serving: 598 calories, 25 g total fat (14 g saturated fat), 86 mg cholesterol, 596 mg sodium, 66 g carbohydrate, 3 g fiber, 28 g protein. Daily Value: 57% vitamin A, 56% vitamin C, 42% calcium, 22% iron.

MUSHROOM AND BARLEY PILAF

Don't be surprised—the barley almost triples while it cooks, making this a hearty main dish.

2   cups sliced fresh mushrooms
4   green onions, sliced (½ cup)
1   medium carrot, shredded (½ cup)
½   teaspoon bottled minced garlic
1   tablespoon margarine or butter
1   14½-ounce can vegetable broth
      or chicken broth
1½   cups quick-cooking barley
1   teaspoon dried basil, oregano, or
      marjoram, crushed, or ½ teaspoon
      dried sage, crushed
¼   teaspoon coarsely ground pepper
1   6-ounce package frozen pea pods
½   cup pecan halves

In a medium saucepan cook mushrooms, green onions, carrot, and garlic in hot margarine or butter over medium heat till mushrooms are tender. Stir in broth; barley; basil, oregano, marjoram, or sage; and pepper. Bring to boiling. Reduce heat. Cover and simmer for 15 to 18 minutes or till barley is tender and liquid is absorbed.

Meanwhile, place frozen pea pods in a colander. Run cold water over the pea pods for 1 to 2 minutes or till thawed. Drain.

Stir pea pods and pecans into barley mixture. Cover. Let stand for 2 to 3 minutes or till heated through. Transfer to a serving bowl. Sprinkle with pecans. Makes 4 servings.

Nutrition facts per serving: 414 calories, 14 g total fat (1 g saturated fat), 0 mg cholesterol, 480 mg sodium, 67 g carbohydrate, 9 g fiber, 11 g protein. Daily Value: 66% vitamin A, 22% vitamin C, 3% calcium, 21% iron.

ITALIAN THREE-BEAN AND RICE SKILLET
Red beans, lima beans, and green beans comprise the basil-scented trio.

1 15- to 15½-ounce can small red
   beans or red kidney beans, rinsed
   and drained
1 14½-ounce can Italian-style stewed
   tomatoes, cut up
1 cup vegetable broth or chicken broth
¾ cup quick-cooking brown rice
½ of a 10-ounce package frozen baby
   lima beans
½ of a 9-ounce package frozen cut
   green beans
½ teaspoon dried basil, crushed, or dried
   Italian seasoning, crushed
1 cup meatless spaghetti sauce
2 ounces thinly sliced mozzarella cheese
   or ¼ cup grated Parmesan cheese
   (optional)

In a large skillet combine red beans or kidney beans, *undrained* tomatoes, broth, rice, lima beans, green beans, and basil or Italian seasoning. Bring to boiling. Reduce heat. Cover and simmer about 15 minutes or till rice is tender.

Stir in spaghetti sauce. Heat through. Top with mozzarella or Parmesan cheese, if desired. Makes 4 servings.

Nutrition facts per serving: 259 calories, 4 g total fat (0 g saturated fat), 0 mg cholesterol, 1103 mg sodium, 50 g carbohydrate, 10 g fiber, 14 g protein. Daily Value: 18% vitamin A, 48% vitamin C, 78% calcium, 19% iron.

PASTA AND PEAS AU GRATIN

Another time, try bite-size pieces of fresh asparagus instead of the peas. Just add them to the pasta during the last 3 to 4 minutes of cooking time.

1   9-ounce package refrigerated cheese-
    filled tortellini or cheese-filled
    ravioli
1   cup frozen peas
2   tablespoons all-purpose flour
⅛   teaspoon pepper
1   cup half-and-half, light cream, or milk
1   14-ounce can chunky tomatoes with
    garlic and spices
2   tablespoons finely shredded Parmesan
    cheese

In a large saucepan cook tortellini or ravioli according to package directions, *except* add peas for the last 1 minute of cooking. Drain. Return pasta mixture to the hot saucepan.

Meanwhile, in a medium saucepan stir together flour and pepper. Gradually stir in half-and-half, light cream, or milk. Cook and stir over medium heat till thickened and bubbly. Cook and stir for 1 minute more. Gradually stir in the *undrained* tomatoes. Pour over pasta. Toss to coat. Sprinkle with Parmesan cheese. Makes 4 servings.

Nutrition facts per serving: 433 calories, 15 g total fat (5 g saturated fat), 25 mg cholesterol, 1098 mg sodium, 55 g carbohydrate, 1 g fiber, 18 g protein. **Daily Value:** *18% vitamin A, 25% vitamin C, 29% calcium, 11% iron.*

SPINACH-FETA FRITTATA

Freeze any leftover feta cheese. Because it's a crumbly cheese, the texture changes little when frozen. Wrap tightly in freezer wrap and thaw in the refrigerator before using.

6 slightly beaten eggs
¼ cup milk
1 teaspoon dried dillweed
¼ teaspoon salt
¼ teaspoon pepper
1 medium onion, chopped (½ cup)
½ teaspoon bottled minced garlic
1 tablespoon margarine or butter
½ of a 10-ounce package frozen chopped
    spinach, thawed
¼ teaspoon lemon-pepper seasoning
¼ cup crumbled feta cheese (1 ounce)

In a medium mixing bowl combine eggs, milk, dillweed, salt, and pepper. Set aside.

In a 10-inch broilerproof skillet cook onion and garlic in hot margarine or butter till tender. Stir in spinach and lemon-pepper seasoning.

Pour egg mixture into the skillet over spinach mixture. Cook over medium heat. As mixture sets, run a spatula around the edge of the skillet, lifting egg mixture to allow uncooked portions to flow underneath. Continue cooking and lifting edges till egg mixture is almost set (surface will be moist).

Sprinkle with feta cheese. Place broilerproof skillet under the broiler 4 to 5 inches from the heat. Broil for 1 to 2 minutes or till top is just set. Cut into 8 wedges. Makes 4 servings.

Nutrition facts per serving: 206 calories, 14 g total fat (5 g saturated fat), 335 mg cholesterol, 536 mg sodium, 6 g carbohydrate, 0 g fiber, 13 g protein.
Daily Value: 39% vitamin A, 7% vitamin C, 25% calcium, 11% iron.

PASTA-FRUIT SALAD

This refreshing salad might surprise you as a main dish, but the pasta, cheese, and nuts team up to provide plenty of protein.

4 ounces ruffle pasta, medium shell macaroni, or corkscrew macaroni (rotini)

1 16-ounce can apricot halves in light syrup or one 16-ounce can peach slices in light syrup, drained

1 8-ounce can pineapple tidbits (juice pack) or one 11-ounce can mandarin orange sections, drained

1 cup seedless red or green grapes, halved

¾ cup shredded cheddar cheese (3 ounces)

¼ cup broken pecans or walnuts

½ of an 8-ounce container vanilla yogurt

1 tablespoon frozen orange juice concentrate

⅛ teaspoon ground nutmeg
  Lettuce leaves

Cook pasta according to package directions. Drain. Rinse with cold water. Drain again.

Meanwhile, cut up apricot halves or peach slices. In a large bowl toss together apricots or peaches, pineapple tidbits or orange sections, grapes, cheese, and pecans or walnuts. Add pasta. Toss to mix. Place in freezer till serving time (up to 30 minutes).

For dressing, stir together yogurt, orange juice concentrate, and nutmeg. Add dressing to pasta mixture; toss to coat. Line four salad plates with lettuce leaves. Divide salad among lettuce-lined plates. Makes 4 servings.

Nutrition facts per serving: 411 calories, 13 g total fat (5 g saturated fat), 24 mg cholesterol, 163 mg sodium, 65 g carbohydrate, 3 g fiber, 12 g protein. Daily Value: 23% vitamin A, 14% vitamin C, 18% calcium, 14% iron.

CHEESY EGG WEDGES

This dish is perfect for a quick supper or a leisurely brunch. You also can cut it into 16 wedges and serve it as an appetizer.

4   beaten eggs
⅓   cup milk
¼   cup all-purpose flour
½   teaspoon baking powder
⅛   teaspoon garlic powder
2   cups shredded cheddar or mozzarella
       cheese (8 ounces)
1   cup cream-style cottage cheese
       with chives
1   cup meatless spaghetti sauce or salsa
     Fresh basil (optional)

In a medium mixing bowl combine eggs, milk, flour, baking powder, and garlic powder. Beat with a rotary beater till combined. Stir in cheddar or mozzarella cheese and cottage cheese.

Pour into a greased 9-inch pie plate. Bake, uncovered, in a 375° oven for 25 to 30 minutes or till golden and a knife inserted near center comes out clean.

Meanwhile, in a small saucepan warm spaghetti sauce or salsa over medium-low heat about 5 minutes or till warm, stirring occasionally.

To serve, cut egg mixture into 6 wedges. Top with spaghetti sauce or salsa. Garnish with fresh basil, if desired. Makes 6 servings.

Nutrition facts per serving: 273 calories, 18 g total fat (10 g saturated fat), 186 mg cholesterol, 614 mg sodium, 9 g carbohydrate, 0 g fiber, 20 g protein. Daily Value: 25% vitamin A, 20% vitamin C, 30% calcium, 9% iron.

RICE 'N' BEAN TOSTADOS

Quick-cooking brown rice, canned chili beans, and a package of mixed salad greens make quick work of these tostados.

1½   cups water
1½   cups quick-cooking brown rice
 1   medium onion, chopped (½ cup)
 1   15-ounce can chili beans with
      chili gravy
 1   8-ounce can whole kernel corn,
      drained
 4   9- to 10-inch flour tortillas
 3   cups torn mixed salad greens
½   cup shredded cheddar cheese
      (2 ounces)
¼   cup dairy sour cream
 1   medium tomato, chopped (⅔ cup)

In a large saucepan bring water to boiling. Stir in rice and onion. Return to boiling. Reduce heat. Cover and simmer for 5 minutes. Remove from heat. Stir. Let stand, covered, for 5 minutes. Stir *undrained* chili beans and corn into rice mixture. Heat through.

Meanwhile, place tortillas on a large baking sheet, overlapping as necessary. Bake in a 400° oven about 10 minutes or till tortillas begin to brown around the edges.

Place each tortilla on a dinner plate. Top tortillas with salad greens and the rice-bean mixture. Sprinkle with cheddar cheese. Serve with sour cream and chopped tomato. Makes 4 servings.

Nutrition facts per serving: 512 calories, 14 g total fat (6 g saturated fat), 21 mg cholesterol, 735 mg sodium, 81 g carbohydrate, 9 g fiber, 19 g protein. Daily Value: 23% vitamin A, 37% vitamin C, 20% calcium, 26% iron.

CHEESY CORN CHOWDER

American cheese gives this creamy soup its velvety texture.

1 14½-ounce can chicken broth
1 10-ounce package frozen whole
    kernel corn
1 4½-ounce can diced green chili
    peppers, drained
½ teaspoon chili powder
2 cups milk
3 tablespoons all-purpose flour
1 cup shredded American cheese
    (4 ounces)
   Parsley (optional)

In a large saucepan combine broth, corn, chili peppers, and chili powder. Bring to boiling. Reduce heat. Cover and simmer 5 minutes.

Gradually stir the milk into the flour till combined. Stir milk mixture into hot mixture in the saucepan. Cook and stir over medium heat till mixture is slightly thickened and bubbly. Cook and stir for 1 minute more. Add cheese, stirring till melted. Ladle into soup bowls. Garnish with parsley, if desired. Makes 4 servings.

Nutrition facts per serving: 273 calories, 13 g total fat (7 g saturated fat), 36 mg cholesterol, 878 mg sodium, 27 g carbohydrate, 0 g fiber, 16 g protein. Daily Value: 20% vitamin A, 22% vitamin C, 30% calcium, 8% iron.

Keep track of your daily nutrition needs by using the information we provide at the end of each recipe. We've analyzed the nutritional content of each recipe serving for you. When a recipe gives an ingredient substitution, we used the first choice in the analysis. If it makes a range of servings (such as 4 to 6), we used the smallest number. Ingredients listed as optional weren't included in the calculations.

METRIC COOKING HINTS

By making a few conversions, cooks in Australia, Canada, and the United Kingdom can use the recipes in Better Homes and Gardens® *30-Minute Main Dishes* with confidence. The charts on this page provide a guide for converting measurements from the U.S. customary system, which is used throughout this book, to the imperial and metric systems. There also is a conversion table for oven temperatures to accommodate the differences in oven calibrations.

Volume and Weight: Americans traditionally use cup measures for liquid and solid ingredients. The chart (top right) shows the approximate imperial and metric equivalents. If you are accustomed to weighing solid ingredients, here are some helpful approximate equivalents.
■ 1 cup butter, caster sugar, or rice = 8 ounces = about 250 grams
■ 1 cup flour = 4 ounces = about 125 grams
■ 1 cup icing sugar = 5 ounces = about 150 grams
Spoon measures are used for smaller amounts of ingredients. Although the size of the tablespoon varies slightly among countries, for practical purposes and for recipes in this book, a straight substitution is all that's necessary.
Measurements made using cups or spoons should always be level, unless stated otherwise.

Product Differences: Most of the ingredients called for in the recipes in this book are available in English-speaking countries. However, some are known by different names. Here are some common American ingredients and their possible counterparts:
■ Sugar is granulated or caster sugar.
■ Powdered sugar is icing sugar.
■ All-purpose flour is plain household flour or white flour. When self-rising flour is used in place of all-purpose flour in a recipe that calls for leavening, omit the leavening agent (baking soda or baking powder) and salt.
■ Light corn syrup is golden syrup.
■ Cornstarch is cornflour.
■ Baking soda is bicarbonate of soda.
■ Vanilla is vanilla essence.
■ Green, red or yellow sweet peppers are capsicums.
■ Sultanas are golden raisins.

USEFUL EQUIVALENTS: U.S = AUST./BR.

⅛ teaspoon = 0.5 ml
¼ teaspoon = 1 ml
½ teaspoon = 2 ml
1 teaspoon = 5 ml
1 tablespoon = 1 tablespoon
¼ cup = 2 tablespoons = 2 fluid ounces = 60 ml
⅓ cup = ¼ cup = 3 fluid ounces = 90 ml
½ cup = ⅓ cup = 4 fluid ounces = 120 ml
⅔ cup = ½ cup = 5 fluid ounces = 150 ml
¾ cup = ⅔ cup = 6 fluid ounces = 180 ml
1 cup = ¾ cup = 8 fluid ounces = 240 ml
1¼ cups = 1 cup
2 cups = 1 pint
1 quart = 1 litre
½ inch = 1.27 centimetres
1 inch = 2.54 centimetres

BAKING PAN SIZES

American	Metric
8x1½-inch round baking pan	20x4-centimetre cake tin
9x1½-inch round baking pan	23x3.5-centimetre cake tin
11x7x1½-inch baking pan	28x18x4-centimetre baking tin
13x9x2-inch baking pan	30x20x3-centimetre baking tin
2-quart rectangular baking dish	30x20x3-centimetre baking tin
15x10x2-inch baking pan	30x25x2-centimetre baking tin (Swiss roll tin)
9-inch pie plate	22x4- or 23x4-centimetre pie plate
7- or 8-inch springform pan	18- or 20-centimetre springform or loose-bottom cake tin
9x5x3-inch loaf pan	23x13x7-centimetre or 2-pound narrow loaf tin or paté tin
1½-quart casserole	1.5-litre casserole
2-quart casserole	2-litre casserole

OVEN TEMPERATURE EQUIVALENTS

Fahrenheit Setting	Celsius Setting*	Gas Setting
300°F	150°C	Gas Mark 2 (slow)
325°F	160°C	Gas Mark 3 (moderately slow)
350°F	180°C	Gas Mark 4 (moderate)
375°F	190°C	Gas Mark 5 (moderately hot)
400°F	200°C	Gas Mark 6 (hot)
425°F	220°C	Gas Mark 7
450°F	230°C	Gas Mark 8 (very hot)
Broil		Grill

Electric and gas ovens may be calibrated using Celsius. However, increase the Celsius setting 10 to 20 degrees when cooking above 160°C with an electric oven. For convection or forced-air ovens (gas or electric), lower the temperature setting 10°C when cooking at all heat levels.